The S.W.A.N. Concept

The S.W.A.N. Concept

SLEEP WELL AT NIGHT, BEFORE AND AFTER RETIREMENT

Robert J. Duchin
with Amy Buttell

ISBN-13: 9781979927888
ISBN-10: 197992788X
Library of Congress Control Number: 2017918349
CreateSpace Independent Publishing Platform
North Charleston, South Carolina
Licensed Insurance Professional. This material has been provided by a licensed insurance professional
for informational and educational purposes only and is not endorsed or affiliated with the Social
Security Administration or any government agency. It is not intended to provide, and should not
be relied upon for, accounting, legal, tax or investment advice.

Securities offered through Robert J. Duchin as a Registered Representative of World Capital
Brokerage, Inc.

This book is dedicated to my wife, Patty, who has been the best support a husband could imagine for forty-seven years; our daughter Missy, whom I adore with all my heart and soul; and in the memory of our daughter Robyn who brought so much love and happiness to my life.

About the Author

Robert J. Duchin began his career in 1970 following graduation from Robert Morris College, with a degree in business administration and management. He founded Robert J. Duchin & Associates Ltd., located outside of Pittsburgh in Harrison City, Pennsylvania, to help individuals and businesses with financial strategies.

Bob also offers insurance and annuity products for middle- and high-tax-bracket individuals and families as well as corporate clients. Led by founder and president Bob Duchin, Robert J. Duchin & Associates Ltd. recognizes a deep responsibility in helping clients and people who need assistance in different areas of financial services.

Robert J. Duchin & Associates Ltd.'s objective is very simple but vital: to help clients who need professional financial advice and strategies so that they can maintain a stable, protected, and predictable lifestyle in their working years and during retirement. With more than forty-five years of experience, Bob believes in continuous study and research to discover effective strategies for individual client needs. He works closely with CPAs, attorneys, and trust officers in applying their joint expertise to the financial problems at hand. Bob practices professionalism by staying in close touch with his clients, responding quickly to their requests and following through on all of his commitments.

Through his membership in the International Association of Registered Financial Consultants (IARFC), Bob holds the designation of Registered Financial Consultant (RFC). This organization confers this designation on financial representatives who meet the high standards of education, experience, and integrity that are membership requirements. Bob is also an approved member of the National

Ethics Bureau, an independent organization that promotes consumer confidence by providing a one-stop source for consumers interested in verifying the business ethics of insurance and financial advisors. All approved members must successfully pass the Ethics Check System, a series of seven-year background checks for criminal, civil, and business violations.

Bob has also been awarded the professional designation of Certified Estate Planner (CEP) from the National Institute of Certified Financial Planners. The CEP designation is held by thousands of professionals in the United States and around the world who use their expertise to help US citizens all over the world. Attorneys, CPAs, financial advisors, and insurance brokers who are dedicated to helping individuals and families with their estate plans hold this designation.

A critical part of Bob's success is his ability to communicate and connect with people. Bob never forgets his clients. Regardless of the question, Bob can track down the answer. Bob realizes that service after the sale is as important as the sale itself. He connects with clients regularly through the phone, through in-person meetings, and by letter.

Robert J. Duchin & Associates Ltd. is equipped with the ability and know-how to answer your timely financial questions, such as the following:

- Are tax-advantaged investments right for me?
- Am I getting the maximum retirement benefits from my pension program?
- Do I have enough life insurance?
- Will my estate have any taxes to pay when I die?

These are just a few of the questions that his clients ask. If you don't know the answers to these and other questions, chances are Bob can help you. Throughout the decades he has operated in the financial and insurance industries, Bob has lectured throughout the country on various topics dealing with financial services. He has also written articles that have appeared in insurance and financial publications.

Bob is a qualifying and life member of the Million Dollar Round Table, with many years of qualification in the elite club known as the Court of the Table, an honor reserved for the industry's top performers. He is the recipient of the National Quality Award, one of the insurance industry's most coveted awards from the National Association of Insurance and Financial Advisors. This award is given to qualified individuals demonstrating consistent and quality production. Bob has also received the National Sales Achievement Award many times throughout his career.

Bob is also a licensed insurance broker and is able to provide clients with products to help achieve their financial goals.

Insurance, estate planning, and retirement strategies are concepts that have come to the forefront of the banking, insurance, investment, and brokerage industries. Federal income-tax laws are complex and subject to change. Neither the company nor its representatives gives legal or tax advice. Please consult your attorney or tax advisors to answer specific questions.

Client Testimonials

During a forty-seven-year-long career, I've worked with many individuals. I am fortunate that most of the people who became clients early in my career are still with me today, and I am proud to say that some of them have become lifelong friends as well. Below are some statements from a few of these people regarding the quality of my service as well as the friendships that we have developed over the years.

Paul Miret

I've known Bob for more than twelve years. What stands out about Bob is how he stays on top of the industry, his personal service, and the fact that he owns the products that he sells—he puts his money where his mouth is. Bob is my eyes and ears into what is happening in the financial and insurance industries. When he makes a recommendation, I take it very seriously because I know how well informed he is. Unlike other financial advisors and insurance agents, Bob is very diligent about staying in touch after a sale. I hear from him regularly. His standard of service sets him apart from the rest of the industry. Bob treats each one of us like his own client and really looks out for our welfare. I consider him a dear friend.

Marc Allen, MD

I met Bob more than thirty years ago when I was a resident at Mt. Sinai Hospital. I attended a financial-workshop presentation he gave and was quite impressed.

When I came back to Mt. Sinai in a role that put me in charge of resident education, Bob was one of the people I tapped to help provide financial information. He is incredibly knowledgeable and generous with his time, driving up to Cleveland from Pittsburgh to give professional presentations that provided information that they really needed.

On a personal basis, Bob has been so helpful in terms of explaining the benefits of the products he has sold to my wife and me that have made a big difference in our lives. I had been told by others that term life insurance was the way to go, but when Bob explained the benefits of whole life insurance, my wife and I purchased that insurance, and we now have a significant amount of capital in our policies. Bob also sold me a disability policy that I never thought I would use. My wife wasn't always sure of the value, and the premiums aren't cheap. But after a heart attack, knee replacement, and back surgery, I was unable to practice. The disability policy has paid monthly income that we otherwise wouldn't have.

Bob has helped us tremendously. I count him as a valued member of the financial team that I have helping us out with our finances, estate planning, taxes, and other matters. He has always provided us with good advice. Now that I am in my early sixties, I have more concern about a potential market blowup, and Bob has been very helpful in diversifying our retirement investments so that our retirement hasn't been as exposed to as much risk. Bob is an incredible professional— there is no one more detailed oriented and who follows up more than Bob. His example has helped me become more professional, because I have learned by watching how he goes about his business.

Alvin (Tagg) Murn, MD

I actually met Bob when I was in medical school; a friend of mine referred me to him. I liked him immediately. He is a wonderful person, very warm and confident. Our relationship started out on a professional basis but turned into a friendship. He is very trustworthy. I have referred friends to Bob because I believe that while you might find someone as good, there is no one better. He is at the top of his game. Bob is an incredibly ethical person. I would trust him with anything insurance or financial related. He is a consummate professional and an incredible friend—I am proud to know him.

Here is a story that tells you something very important about Bob. When I moved to North Carolina, he extended himself to get a North Carolina insurance license. He didn't have to, but he did it because I moved here, and he wanted to ensure that he could continue to help me. Bob is also a natural teacher—he explains everything very clearly and has always been dead on right about the markets and the products he has sold.

Rick Florek

Bob has a huge heart—I consider him a friend; our relationship is much more than business. He gets to know your family and is very caring. I got to know him through golf and then started doing business with him, and then we became good friends. He would do anything for his friends. He has been a big help to me with annuities so that I will have a stable financial environment when I get to the point of retiring and needing steady income. He is one of the most generous people I know.

Len Selednik, MD

I met Bob in 1976, the year I got married, the bicentennial. So we've known each other for more than forty years. Bob has an effervescent personality—he is very outgoing, and we got along well from the very beginning. Bob doesn't pull his punches or hold back from expressing himself. He has a lot of energy and always goes far beyond the call of duty to help his clients. He always follows through and never drops the ball. His strengths include his willingness to help and his desire to communicate frequently with his clients. Whenever I meet with Bob, I get a follow-up letter a few days later, reviewing our conversation and helping me appreciate the context and benefits of whatever financial product we've been discussing. Bob never pushes—he helps you understand what opportunities are out there that you don't want to miss. He keeps his explanations simple, always making sure that my wife and I know what we need to know. He is not one to cut corners, bend the truth, or skirt any ethical standards. He couldn't sleep well at night if he did that.

Bob's strong suit is friendship, helping people feel liked, appreciated, and valued. In terms of our professional relationship, Bob's style runs parallel to that of me and my wife—we want to be careful of risk so that we can sleep well at night. During the past five years, the products that Bob put us in really hit their stride, and we have little or no anxiety about the future. Bob is a unique financial advisor in terms of his forthrightness, his clarity of communication, his simplicity of style, and his integrity. I would say he is one of the most avid keepers of integrity I know.

Tim Shepherd

I've known Bob for the past ten years. We started out as golfing acquaintances, and during that time, he never approached me about my finances. I think that is admirable because many financial advisors belong to this club, and they are always prospecting, if not on the course, after a game or through a follow-up e-mail. In fact, I approached him to open up a discussion about financial advising and financial matters. He is a no-pressure guy—I trust him 100 percent and am very comfortable with all the business I have done with him. He is a very caring individual. He is someone I respect, and I would never hesitate to throw his name out if a friend was seeking someone to help with their finances and retirement investing. Over the years, I have found that Bob offers incredibly efficient service—basically, I would tell my friends that there is no one that would provide a higher level of service than Bob. He gives you all the information you need to make a decision and makes sure that all question are answered. I trust him with my investments more than I have trusted anyone that I have ever worked with. Like Bob, I am more of a squirrel in my investing approach in terms of saving for a rainy day and not wanting to court too much risk, so the SWAN theory—sleep well at night—works very well for me. In fact, I have a plastic swan in my office that Bob gave me, and I see it every day on my desk and think about him.

Marci Suggars

I began working for Bob when I was twenty-one, in 1983. One thing that hasn't changed is his passion for client service. It has been such a pleasure over the years to see how his young, struggling clients, many of whom were medical students and residents, have now reached a high level of success. With Bob's conservative guidance, these doctors, entrepreneurs, and executives are in a great position in their financial lives, enjoying the fruits of their hard work. There are so many keys to Bob's success, including his organization, efficiency, knowledge, and compassion. He would never ever consider selling a product that he wasn't familiar with himself, that he didn't know through and through. He will not get involved in anything risky—I tell my friends and family that if he is putting money into something, it is a good thing for you; it will be protected because he doesn't like risk. I consider Bob the most successful man I know. I call him our financial guardian angel. Bob provides us all with a financial-security blanket. He remembers where he came from and is very down-to-earth. I love working with him. Bob's influence has made me who I am today—I am a better person, a better volunteer, and a better parent for having worked with and known Bob. Most people who know him feel that way—he has impacted so many people and inspired them to be more ethical, more successful, and to work harder. On a personal note, I want to add that almost three years ago, after thirty-one years of marriage to my high-school sweetheart, I unexpectedly became a fifty-two-year-old widow. My husband had a successful career, and I was the beneficiary of his group-life-insurance and 401(k) proceeds. I immediately turned to Bob to see how this money would best serve me and my young daughter. I can proudly say that although I have a lot of concerns about my future, my finances are not one of them. I truly do *sleep well at night*. Thanks to Bob's guidance.

Barbara Wilhelm, MD

I became acquainted with Bob through my late husband. I would tell anyone who is considering doing business with him, receiving financial help from him, that he is extremely dedicated and trustworthy. He has always provided good advice and gets back to me immediately. He has been very helpful to me personally. I have found Bob's advice to be very sound. He works to get his clients in a position where we don't have to worry about the market impacting our savings. You can't control volatility in the market, and I am glad to be invested in products, such as deferred annuities, where you aren't exposed to the market. Bob is a very genuine person, very service oriented, almost Type A, which is what you want in a financial advisor. If I have a question, he answers it immediately. Even if I am not in a hurry, he will always get back to me quickly. Some service people are not dependable, and then it is hard to feel confident. Bob is a person who is very responsive and communicative.

Larry Gipson, MD

I have known Bob for more than thirty years, and usually over time, a person's true self will come out. During those thirty years, Bob has never disappointed, never not kept his word, and always delivered more than what he promised. I would recommend Bob to anyone. He is a consummate professional, and he serves his interests by serving his clients' interests first.

Tom Mayrides

I consider myself relatively astute about investments, but when I went to Bob for advice on annuities, he knew much more about the subject than I did. He structured a situation for me that was perfect for my needs at that time. Bob is different from many financial advisors in that he presents information and facts and isn't trying to push a sale. He analyzes each client's individual situation and structures something tailored for that person, not to make a fast buck. I have referred him to two friends and wouldn't hesitate to refer him again. He is incredibly trustworthy, professional, and diligent. His business philosophy wouldn't permit him to sell something that he didn't strongly feel was suitable for a specific client based on their needs.

Chuck Dugan, MD

I met Bob more than twenty years ago, and he helped us get set up with a disability policy. When I was diagnosed with cancer two years ago, the disability policy ensured that my family was taken care of, which was important, especially since we have a daughter still in college. Bob has become a great friend. I would highly recommend him to anyone. He provides a very high level of service and is very personable. I recently transitioned my retirement savings into annuities because of his advice, because I don't want to take the risk with everything happening in the market and in Washington. Because of all of Bob's help, our estate plan is in order with the estate-planning attorney he recommended. It is so important to have that in place, especially because of my cancer. I am very pleased that it is all established so we don't have to worry about that.

Judith Wolkoff

I would absolutely recommend Bob to anyone who is interested in getting financial advice. We have been with him for more than thirty-eight years. We started with life insurance to protect our family, and because we were just starting out and didn't have much money, Bob put us in a program that fit our situation perfectly. Bob has never steered us wrong. I haven't always understood finances or investments, but Bob explains everything clearly and is a very genuine person who is very trustworthy. When he tells us something isn't a good move for us, I trust that it isn't. He has kept us and our financial situation moving forward for nearly forty years. When I retired last year, he recommended that I place my retirement savings in annuities due to the safety and lack of risk, which I agree with—I don't want to lose money in a market crash when I'm not in a position to make it up because of not making an income anymore. Bob is a very enthusiastic, positive person who is always responsive to my calls. He explains things in a way that we can understand. When we needed to change our estate plans, he and his assistant, Marci, were incredibly helpful. I trust that Bob will always steer us right.

Section 1
The Front Nine

CHAPTER 1
The Beginning

'm Bob Duchin, and my job is to help my clients and their families sleep well at night, not worrying about income in retirement. During the past forty-seven years, I've built a financial-advisory practice around helping those clients find financial protection during all stages of life. I believe there is no more important task than helping doctors, executives, and entrepreneurs preserve their hard-earned money so that they and their families can enjoy the financial freedom they desire.

It's been my privilege to serve many of the same clients for decades. I pride myself on the fact that many clients have become my friends. I still have a number of clients whom I first met when they were in medical school, internship, residency, and the earliest years of practice. In a sense, we grew our careers alongside each other and now are entering a period in our lives where financial protection is more important than ever because retirement is looming. Throughout that period, my philosophy of helping clients protect their families, their earnings, and their savings hasn't changed. I don't like risk and do everything I can to provide my clients with conservative guidance and advice that will preserve their savings.

Growing a Career and Family

In those years, many of these young doctors got married and started having children all while building their practices. I was already married to my wife Patty, and we grew our family through the addition of two beautiful daughters. Those were busy years—doctors' schedules being what they are, I would meet with them in the evenings, on weekends, in between shifts in the emergency room, and after long days spent in the operating room. As I considered their situations and determined the most appropriate financial strategy, I noticed a common denominator. These young doctors were determined to protect their families while building wealth for the future. They worked long hours and wanted to ensure that should something happen to them, their spouses and children would be free of financial worry.

What implications did that have for the financial products they were interested in? In other words, what financial products were going to help these young doctors provide for their families in the way they intended? Clearly, life insurance and disability insurance fit that need. Now, I've been a financial advisor since 1970, and I've seen all sorts of financial trends come and go. I have a securities license, and I am licensed to sell securities and insurance in a number of states, including Pennsylvania and Florida. There are a lot of products I can sell and have sold. My goal, as I searched for the most suitable policies, was to match their individual situations and desire to protect their families in the event of some unforeseen catastrophe with the most appropriate insurance product possible.

While there weren't nearly as many different types of financial products in the 1970s and 1980s as there are now, there were many different insurance companies. Those companies offered a variety of life and insurance policies. I've always had an aptitude for learning and continuing education, and in these years, that attribute came in handy. In a constant whirl of meetings, conversations, and phone calls, I also spent hours at my desk in reading financial, investing, and insurance material and policies and spent days out of the office on trips designed to increase my knowledge and awareness of insurance products and the different ways those products could help my clients and prospective clients.

There is no one-size-fits-all client, just as there is no-one-size-fits-all insurance policy. Every client and every client situation is unique and demands an individualized approach. Just because Dr. Jones just purchased a whole life-insurance policy does not mean that same policy, or even a whole life-insurance policy, is right for Dr. Smith.

The Fact-Finding Process

That is why I typically have two or three conversations with a prospective or even a current client. I need to fully understand their current financial situation—that includes their income, their savings, their investments, and their goals. Through this fact-finding process, I ask clients to bring me their bank, investment, and financial statements so I can build a comprehensive picture of their finances. I take time going over those documents so I can understand where they currently are and where they want to go. Only then do I begin considering all the potential products that I have at my disposal and which types of products would be the most suitable.

So I start there. If, after I have talked to a client and his or her spouse, it is evident that they want to protect their family from a possible future tragedy, the best answer is life insurance. Whether whole or term, or which type of whole or term is better, depends on their goals, their budget, and their time horizon. If the goal is for the doctor, executive, or entrepreneur to hedge against a potential disability, then disability insurance is clearly the most appropriate option. Which type of disability policy depends, again, on the individual client's situation, needs, budget, and goals.

My point is that my years of experience and in-depth knowledge of products ensures that I match my clients with a financial product that meets their needs. An important part of that process is education, which includes relaying the information to my clients. I always do my best to ensure my clients understand the ins and outs of the products they are purchasing. I am proud to report that if a client decides to purchase a financial product, I fill out those applications myself. I believe it is my responsibility to ensure that the application is correct and that clients have received all the appropriate disclosures and information they need as part of the process of purchasing an insurance policy or annuity. I am never too busy to take a phone call and explain a specific clause of a policy or make a change to a policy that is being written. The meetings I hold with clients and their spouses are designed to ensure that they both understand what they are purchasing, the product's fees and costs, and what it is designed to do for them.

The Shift toward Retirement Savings

My methodical, organized approach to client service served me well as many of my clients moved closer to retirement because I was able to help them in the most appropriate way. The needs of these young doctors, executives, and entrepreneurs have evolved as they have progressed in their careers, gaining promotions and amassing wealth. Now they are more interested in protecting their retirement and providing a legacy for their family. Of course, saving for retirement isn't something that the vast majority of them have waited to do—they have saved throughout their whole careers. They are at the point in their lives where their focus has moved from growing their wealth through savings and investing to preserving it.

That is completely in alignment with my investing philosophy and how I personally invest. I really don't like risk. While the stock market certainly has the potential to deliver high returns, it also can devastate a portfolio. We all remember 2008, during the height of the financial crisis, when the S&P 500 lost 38.5 percent in one year.[1] Think about that—if you had invested $100,000 on January 1, 2008, and held that through the end of the year, your investment would have been worth $61,500 on December 31. If that happened the year you decided to retire, it could potentially devastate your income stream in retirement, forcing you to abandon plans for vacations, spending time with your family and hobbies. You might even be forced to go back to work! That isn't an acceptable outcome for soon-to-be-retirees who are looking to preserve wealth.

As the need for alternatives that are less risky has emerged, financial products are also evolving. And that's fortunate, because there are products designed to provide protection for investors who don't want to take risks in retirement. For myself, I have found that fixed index annuities are a suitable fit for my objectives. Like many of my clients, I seek guaranteed income in retirement, downside protection, and some growth potential. My wife and I own fifteen annuities, products that will provide a strong stream of guaranteed income throughout retirement. It's important to me that everyone reading this book understand that I would never ever sell an annuity or any other financial product to a client that I did not own myself. There are certain situations where the products I own may not be available to certain clients based on their particular situation. I then shop for the best product for that client's needs.

My clients now own many of the same types of fixed index annuities that I own. These products, and their ability to meet the needs of clients for financial protection, are the focus of this book. I believe fixed index annuities are ideally positioned to meet the needs of many retirees for guaranteed income in retirement, and as you read through this book, you will learn more about these

---

1 "Stock Losses this Year Were Broad based and Dramatic," CNN Money, December 31, 2008, http://money.cnn.com/2008/12/31/markets/SP500_year_end/index.htm?postversion=2008123117 (accessed July 11, 2017)

products and the features that can potentially help you enjoy the retirement you have worked so hard for your entire life.

I'm all about protection. I believe the best possible way to enjoy your retirement is with a feeling of protection regarding your income stream. My goal as a financial advisor and insurance agent is to provide a financial-security blanket for my clients so they can sleep well at night. I like to think of myself as a financial guardian, whom clients can and do call any time they need help and who will be there to do whatever I can to ensure that they achieve their retirement goals and objectives.

CHAPTER 2

Introduction

You can't take a mulligan on retirement—you've got one shot to get it right. And wouldn't it be great if you hit a hole in one?

In my experience, feeling good about your finances in retirement boils down to one simple thing—having enough income to support your lifestyle. The definition of enough income differs depending on the situation of each family. Of course, you need at the minimum enough money to pay your bills such as utilities, any mortgage you may have, gas, food, insurance, unexpected house or car repairs, and other necessities. As you get older, that includes medical expenses such as Medicare Part D, a Medicare Advantage Plan, and even assisted-living or nursing-home care. Those are the basics—then there are the extras, which include travel; visiting with family and friends; entertaining; hobbies such as golf, tennis, and bridge; charitable gifting; and whatever else you've planned on after a life of hard work.

While those essential and extra expenses may differ depending on your specific situation and where you live, what doesn't differ is the need for that income to be consistent. You may not want to wonder every month whether some external factor—like the economy or the stock market—will impact that monthly draw. When you know that you can count on that money to not only pay your bills but also for the fun you want to have in retirement, you can relax and truly enjoy the golden years.

Sources of Retirement Income

For most of us, that monthly income comes from several different sources, which include social security, a pension (if you have one), and your retirement savings.

The federal government will deposit your monthly social-security benefit in your bank account every month. If you have a pension, you can choose a monthly pay-out option that can last a number of years, depending on how much the pension is worth and how long you want to extend the payout.

Then there is the wild card of your retirement savings. If you have a 401(k) or 403(b) plan or a similar plan such as a SEP (Self Employed Retirement Plan), you must take yearly distributions beginning when you turn age seventy and a half. Of course, you can also begin to withdraw money without penalty at age fifty-nine and a half. Many retirees take distributions from these accounts monthly, which are then added to that monthly income stream. However, depending on how that money is invested, that monthly income payout may not be consistent and may not last throughout a long retirement.

That lack of consistency and that nagging fear that you may live longer than your retirement savings can be a tremendous source of insecurity, which has the potential to ruin your retirement or at least interfere with your sleep at night. All too many people are experiencing that reality, riding the rollercoaster of the stock market, feeling more confident when it goes up and possibly terrified when it falls.

And it is not just the stock market. Longevity and inflation are two other unknowns that can imperil your retirement, especially if your monthly income sources aren't stable. It's like trying to get through eighteen holes of golf without knowing in advance how many golf balls or clubs you'll have. It doesn't matter how well you play the front nine (your working years) if you run out of golf balls or clubs on the back nine (your retirement). By ensuring that you have a suffi-cient and guaranteed stream of income that will last, you can relax and enjoy your retirement, just like you can finish that round of golf with the right equipment in your golf bag.

As more of my clients approach retirement, I have spent a great deal of time and energy investigating investment and insurance products in an effort to iden-tify the most suitable approach that will meet their needs for that guaranteed lifetime income stream in retirement. As I've noted, the strategy I've identified and that I have employed in my own retirement planning is fixed index annuities.

An annuity is an insurance product that provides regular income based on the amount of money contributed to that annuity. That amount can range anywhere from $10,000 to $1.5 million or more, depending on your specific financial situa-tion, the specific annuity product, and the company that sells the product. There are two types of fixed annuities: immediate and deferred. Immediate annuities begin generating income immediately or within one year of issue. Deferred annuities, in contrast, postpone the monthly annuity income by as much as ten to twenty years, allowing that premium to grow while you continue to work, providing more income during retirement.

Boost Your Income with Fixed Index Annuities

While there are different kinds of immediate and deferred annuities, I prefer the deferred fixed index annuity. Fixed index annuities' interest calculation is based on a specific formula designed by the issuing insurance company that prevents loss on the downside and provides the opportunity for potential growth. That means you avoid any losses while you still retain the potential to grow the premium. Fixed index annuities give you the opportunity to delay receiving income until you really need it, during retirement.

Flexibility is a great benefit if you aren't sure when you want to retire—you can own one of these products and retire in your sixties or wait until you are in your seventies. In the meantime, if you need some money to renovate your home or buy a car or splurge on a cruise around the world, many annuity contracts permit you to withdraw 5–10 percent a year of the annuity's value. The remaining 90 or 95 percent stays within the annuity, having an opportunity to grow until you are ready to start taking a stream of income when you retire.

What I love about these products is how they produce a sustainable income stream throughout retirement. You need income so you can enjoy those years with your family and pursue those goals you put off during your working years. I work with clients when they decide upon a retirement date to determine how much income they will need to not only pay their expenses but also provide for the activities they want to enjoy, such as travel, hobbies, charitable gifting, and helping their children and grandchildren.

Of course, the amount of monthly income available from a fixed index annuity depends on the initial premium, how long it has grown, and the growth rate. Some fixed-index-annuity providers allow owners to continue to add to their annuity for a period of time, such as a year or longer, and may provide a premium bonus at the time of issue. If that option isn't available or isn't suitable, you can purchase another annuity for yourself, your spouse, or even your grown children.

Create a Worry-Free Retirement

When you add the monthly income that a fixed index annuity can provide to a social-security check and either a pension or income from other investments, you create the basis for a reliable retirement income. Many of my clients have purchased fixed index annuities and are positioning themselves for a postretirement income of $9,000 or $10,000 a month or more. They are thrilled that they won't have to worry about the volatility of the stock market or how long they will live, because they have taken the important step of ensuring that their monthly income will last as long as they need it.

After a lifetime of hard work and saving, you deserve financial freedom. When you know that your expenses are covered in retirement—no matter how long it lasts—you can relax and create a fulfilling experience. For some, that translates into volunteering and charitable gifting. For others, it is spending time with children and grandchildren and building a legacy. Still others yearn to travel the world. Whatever your goal and dream is, I want to help you achieve it. That is why I believe in the SWAN (sleep well at night) concept.

CHAPTER 3
Saving for Retirement

The retirement-savings picture for Americans aged fifty-five and over isn't pretty. In fact, a 2015 federal Government Accountability Office[2] (GAO) study revealed that

- 48 percent have some retirement savings;
- 29 percent have no pension plan or retirement savings; and
- 23 percent have a pension plan but no separate retirement savings.

For those with savings, ages fifty-five to sixty-four, their average savings balance of $104,000 translates into an inflation-protected annuity of $310 a month. Those aged sixty-five to seventy-four are slightly better off with savings of $148,000, translating to a similar annuity worth $649 a month.[3] Clearly, these levels of savings are inadequate to sustain much of any lifestyle in retirement. GAO reports that half of all American households age sixty-five and over obtain approximately half of their income from their monthly social-security check.

Fortunately, my clients and their friends and colleagues aren't in this position. Most have saved all their lives, and their hard work has been rewarded not just with competitive salaries but also with benefits, including retirement plans. Some are fortunate enough to have pensions, also known as defined benefit plans.

---

2 "Retirement Security: Most Households Approaching Retirement Have Low Savings," Government Accountability Office, May 2015, https://www.gao.gov/assets/680/670153.pdf. (July 17, 2017)
3 Ibid. (July 17, 2017)

Savings and Retirement Income

I offer the above statistics to illustrate just how much savings it can take to generate adequate income in retirement. While most established professionals can count on retirement plans through their employers, but with the wild cards of longevity, market risk, and inflation, it can be difficult to know how much you must save to generate stable, guaranteed income during a retirement that can last thirty years or longer. We'll explore those topics in depth in upcoming chapters.

Doctors, entrepreneurs, and executives have plenty of opportunity to save, and most of my clients are type A personalities who want to make sure that their family is protected should something unexpected occur. Many are fortunate enough to have savings in excess of several million dollars, funds accumulated over decades of saving in and out of retirement plans. If they are employed, many save through 401(k) or 403(b) defined contribution plans or profit-sharing plans. If they are self-employed, they usually take advantage of options such as SIMPLE, SEP, or solo 401(k) plans. Many executives at large, publicly traded companies may have stock options that can be exercised and used to finance retirement. Traditional and Roth IRAs are another way to build retirement savings.

There are many situations in which a 401(k), 403(b), or other defined contribution plan can be rolled over into an IRA. These situations include when a professional leaves a job, when a business or practice is closed or terminated, and when the retirement plan itself is terminated. Rolling over one of these plans into an IRA can provide more flexibility with future contribution options, especially those that involve deferred annuities that provide guaranteed income. In the second half of this book, I'll cover how these scenarios can play out for the benefit of your retirement.

Other Savings Goals

Most of these professionals have other savings obligations besides retirement. Midcareer professionals typically juggle a number of savings objectives, including saving for college for their children, saving for a larger house or even a second home, and maintaining an emergency fund to pay for unexpected expenses, such as car and home repairs.

Many are in what is known as the "sandwich" generation, parenting their children as their own parents' age. Some of these elderly parents may need financial assistance from their children, and that can easily become a drain on those adult children unless they plan carefully. In this age of rising medical costs, elderly parents may exhaust their own savings either now or in the future. In addition, adult children may find their own medical expenses rising, especially as high-deductible health plans gain popularity with employers and the overall cost of health care continues to rise.

Even professionals with six-figure or more salaries might be tempted to save less or divert retirement savings to other purposes, such as college tuition for their children. Generally, that isn't a good idea at least until you have the opportunity to evaluate how much savings you have, how much you are on track to save throughout your career, and how that compares to what you should be saving to maintain your lifestyle during retirement.

Transitioning into Retirement

Just like many other Americans, many of these professionals are so focused on their careers and on accumulating wealth for retirement that they likely don't have a clear idea of how those savings will translate into stable, guaranteed income in retirement. Let's face it, in the throes of career building, actual retirement isn't top of mind. Most professionals figure it will take care of itself at the right time. My job is to be there before, during, and after retirement to ensure that all the possible details are taken care of so that transitioning to retirement is as smooth, comfortable, and enjoyable as possible.

This stage of life brings many questions that are worth considering before retirement is actually upon you. You and your spouse, if you have one, need to think about when you both will retire, if you are currently pursuing careers. It can be difficult for one spouse to remain busy with a career while the other one is no longer working. However, that transition, like the entire transition into retirement, can be managed with enough planning and thoughtful conversation.

You will also need to decide if you want to remain living in the city where you live now and in the same house. For some, moving out of the big house where they raised their children and downsizing is liberating, while others want to preserve those memories. Some couples or retiring individuals can't wait to move to a warmer, sunnier, or overall more hospitable climate. Others want to stay put near friends and familiar places. No decision is wrong; it is just best to discuss all this and come to some agreement on it before either of you makes an assumption about retirement that the other one doesn't agree with.

Fitting hobbies, volunteering, traveling, and even part-time work into a retirement schedule is something else to be considered. Some retirees end up going back to work or starting a business because they are bored with too much leisure time, while others so enjoy a slower lifestyle that they wonder how they ever had time to work.

All these factors play into your retirement lifestyle and need to be included in your financial retirement planning process. When I meet with prospective clients or current clients about income in retirement, I conduct a review of their investment and retirement-savings portfolio known as a Fact Finder. At the end of the first section of this book, I will cover that process and how it can help you better understand what you currently own, how your expenses are likely to change between the career years and retirement, how well you are positioned for retirement, and how you can improve your chances of stable retirement income.

CHAPTER 4
Family Protection: Life and Disability Insurance

Professionals can safeguard their families through the simple act of purchasing life and disability insurance as they build their careers. From my perspective, these may be vital coverages for doctors, entrepreneurs, and executives who have invested time, energy, and money in preparing for and pursing their careers.

In my forty-seven years of helping families protect themselves, I've seen many instances of the sacrifices families make during the career-building process. These devoted spouses and children deserve assurance that they will be taken care of in the event of an unexpected occurrence. Let's be honest, many career-minded professionals may spend more time than they would like to away from home to provide a comfortable lifestyle for their families.

When discussing life and disability coverage, I tell my clients that life has three potential outcomes: you live, you die, or you become disabled. Life and disability insurance helps protect you and your family in the event of the outcomes no one wants—death or disability.

Fortunately, life and disability insurance aren't one-size-fits-all products. There are many insurance companies that issue different types of life and disability insurance. I've made a point of staying abreast of developments in the insurance industry over the decades to understand the details of polices and their suitability for my clients as they move through their careers and close in on retirement.

Life Insurance

This is the first situation where I worked with medical students, interns, residents, and young doctors. Aware of the investment that their families had made in their future, they wanted to ensure that their families were protected if they passed away. More than many doctors understand how fragile life is—after all, they dedicate themselves to saving lives and doing no harm when they take the Hippocratic Oath.

While the odds may be in your favor if you decide not to purchase life insurance—life expectancy in the United States being what it is—the fact is that something awful could still happen. Car accidents, cancer, heart attacks, and many other incidents and diseases can rob a healthy professional of his or her life unexpectedly. That's why I recommend life insurance to younger clients—and that isn't just insurance for the main breadwinner. I frequently recommend insurance for both partners in a couple, especially if they are parents. The specifics of those recommendations depend on your individual situation.

If the worst happens, you don't want your family to have to worry about money or scramble to cover expenses. Unfortunately, the death of the main breadwinner can lead to a change in lifestyle if there is no insurance or the policy is insufficient. Many surviving spouses of clients of mine who purchased life insurance years ago have expressed gratitude to me because these policies have helped those families focus on grieving and eventually rebuilding their lives, rather than having to make sudden, destabilizing changes to their lives and living situations while dealing with a devastating bereavement.

What is enough coverage in case of death of the primary breadwinner? Each situation is individual, but a rule of thumb is that a life-insurance policy should be sufficient to pay off a family's debts, supply cash to provide the income previously provided by a salary, and manage future obligations. That looks very different for a family with a large mortgage and young children than it might for an older couple with an empty nest. However, it is best not to underestimate insurance needs as you don't want your family to suffer because you didn't purchase enough insurance.

As you probably already know, there are two main types of life insurance: permanent and term. Permanent life insurance is designed to protect an individual for many years, while term insurance is just what it says—insurance designed to protect you for a specific period, or term, of time. In the next two sections, we'll go over the differences between these two types of insurance and how they can fit into your retirement and legacy plans.

Term Life Insurance

Term life insurance is akin to renting an apartment instead of buying a home. It costs less because at the end of the term, the insurance lapses or is renewed at a different rate for an additional period of time. In other words, when you buy a term policy, you may pay a lower premium for similar coverage, but it's only for a limited time, and you are not building any cash value. The term insurance policy has no cash value once the policy time period expires, just like you have no equity in an apartment you rent when you move out.

Most of my clients who decide on term insurance lock in policies for a ten- to thirty-year term. Term does allow professionals to purchase more insurance for a lower price. However, that's a trade-off—you do get more insurance should something happen to you, but when the policy's term ends, you don't get anything out of it. As a term policy nears its conclusion, I discuss the situation with each client and start looking for another policy, assuming he or she wants to continue coverage. Term is highly flexible coverage that may be suitable for clients who would rather separate their insurance coverage from their investing or who want to obtain a higher level of coverage but don't have the cash flow to support a permanent life policy.

Permanent Life Insurance

In contrast to term insurance, permanent life insurance has a higher premium for similar coverage, but many products have annual dividends designed to help reduce the cost, or they can accumulate to develop future equity. Many contracts also have guaranteed cash values with other potential opportunities for growth to help supplement retirement income.

Role of Life Insurance Later in Life

Once clients have amassed a certain amount of wealth and are moving into the empty-nest, the preretirement stage of life, they may decide to reduce or terminate their permanent or term policies. Their children are likely grown and settled in their own careers and aren't relying on the financial assistance of their parents. These clients may also have sufficient assets in retirement plans, equity in a home, and other investments to take care of a surviving spouse in the event of an untimely death.

Some clients choose to maintain insurance coverage, while others will go ahead and terminate policies, especially term policies. For high-net worth clients whose wealth exceeds the federal estate tax, some choose to transfer or purchase permanent life insurance for life-insurance trusts. Such trusts are used for tax-planning purposes in order to pass wealth on to future generations efficiently. In 2017, the estate tax exemption for individuals is $5.49 million and $10.98 million for couples; in 2018, $5.6 million will be for individuals and $11.2 million for couples, according to the IRS.[4] There is the potential for the estate tax to be repealed in the future, especially as the Trump administration and Congress unveiled several plans in the fall of 2017 to restructure the tax code.[5,6] The status of those was pending at the time of this book's publication.

In cooperation with an experienced estate planning attorney, I help clients assess whether they need to avail themselves of life-insurance trusts and other estate-planning tools. I've developed expertise through a series of courses I took to become a Certified Estate Planner (CEP) from the National Association of Certified Estate Planners.

Disability Insurance

If you experience some type of short-term or long-term disability while still working, your income stream will likely be interrupted. My clients are typically interested in two types of disability insurance:

---

4 "Estate Tax," Internal Revenue Service, October 23, 2017, https://www.irs.gov/businesses/small-businesses-self-employed/estate-tax. (June 28, 2017)

5 "Republican Plan Delivers Permanent Corporate Tax Cut," *The New York Times*, November 2, 2017, https://www.nytimes.com/2017/11/02/us/politics/tax-plan-republicans.html?_r=0. (Nov. 10, 2017)

6 "Senate Republican Tax Plan may Eliminate Property Tax Deductions and Delay Corporate Cut," *Los Angeles Times*, November 7, 2017, http://beta.latimes.com/politics/la-na-pol-gop-tax-plan-20171107-story.html. (Nov. 10, 2017)

- Individual-disability policy: Short- and long-term policies that protect you in case you experience a covered event. Covered events include accidents, illnesses, or conditions that prevent you from working at your regular occupation.
- Business-overhead-expense policy: Short- and long-term policies that protect business owners in the event that they can't perform their jobs. It covers the owner's share of typical business overhead expenses such as rent or mortgage, employee salaries, loan payments, and business supplies.

Typically, I look for disability policies that provide a monthly benefit if the policy owner cannot perform the job that he or she is engaged in. In contrast, some policies will only pay a monthly benefit if the policyholder can't perform any job. For example, if a surgeon injures her hand or wrist and can't perform surgery, she will want a policy that provides a benefit for the period of time that she is unable to work. Otherwise, the insurance company could deny the benefit because there are other occupations she could pursue, such as lecturing at a university, teaching residents, or even acting as a medical expert.

In some cases, disabilities last a lifetime. That's why you want a robust policy that will pay the stipulated benefits if, for whatever reason, you can't work. Imagine if you invested years of your life and considerable resources in gaining expertise in your field and then not being able to work because of a condition that was out of your control. With an appropriate disability policy, you will continue to receive ongoing income to support yourself and your family.

As with life insurance, I recommend regular reviews of disability policies, especially as clients move closer to retirement. Previously, insurance companies would write permanent disability policies, meaning that no matter the age of the policyholder, if he or she was still working, they would receive disability benefits for the rest of his or her life. Recently, however, insurance companies issuing disability policies limit coverage to two years once a policyholder turns age sixty-five. Therefore, some of my clients choose to cancel disability insurance as they get closer to age sixty-five, while others keep it in force as an additional protection.

CHAPTER 5
Don't Let the Market Endanger Your Retirement

've said it before, and I'll say it again. I don't like risk. From my perspective, entrusting your hard-earned retirement savings to the stock market is akin to taking that same money and going gambling at the casino. When you gamble, the deck is stacked in favor of the house. Not only that, but every winning run comes to an end.

While the stock market isn't a casino, there is no predicting what it will do when. Inevitably, bear markets follow bull markets. Heck, you can even have a streak of horrible performance within a bull market. That happened at the beginning of 2016. By the end of January 2016, 93 percent of all stock market investors lost money,[7] according to CNN Money. That same January, the Dow Jones Industrial Average lost 6 percent of its overall value when it fell 1,079 points in one week.[8] Imagine the impact that could have on your portfolio, let alone your confidence.

Volatility Rules the Markets

When it comes to stock markets, volatility isn't the exception; it is the rule. Markets are subject to all sorts of forces, many of them irrational. Even when they are rational,

---

7 "Ouch. 93 Percent of Investors Lost Money in January," CNN Money, February 1, 2016, http://money.cnn.com/2016/02/01/investing/stocks-markets-january-93-percent-lost/index.html. (May 30, 2017)

8 "Historic Week: Dow Plunges 1,079 Points," CNN Money, January 8, 2016, http://money.cnn.com/2016/01/08/investing/stocks-markets-dow-china-oil/. (May 30, 2017)

a down market is a down market, and it will impact your stock portfolio whether the reason for the decline is rational or not. I mentioned the worst downturn in recent memory earlier in this book, which occurred during the Great Recession.

Many of my clients have worked hard in occupations where they are compensated quite well and receive a match on their retirement savings, so as a result, they have accumulated quite a bit of savings. A number of these clients have accumulated between $2 and $3 million in savings, if not more. If you remember, in 2008, the S&P 500 dropped by 37 percent in one year.[9] I want to explore that example in more depth.

In working with clients, I have found that there are three distinct aspects to investment loss—the actual loss of money, the amount of time it takes to regain that loss, and the emotional toll that loss takes. Using the example of a client with $2 to $3 million in retirement savings, if one of those clients had $1 million invested in the S&P 500 at the beginning of 2008, that investment would have been worth $630,000 by the end of that year. That is a loss of $370,000 in one year—and I am sure that it took a considerable number of years to build savings up to that point, only to have that much vanish in just 365 days. I can't imagine having to be the advisor who had to visit or call that client to say that so much money had been lost in just one year.

Now let's look at the second issue, which is how long it would take to rebuild those savings back up to their previous level. You wouldn't be able to get back up to that $1 million if the market magically regained 37 percent. The market would actually have to gain 58 percent just to get you back to where you started. And who knows how long that would take and if you would have time to wait? Meanwhile, you might actually need that money in retirement. If you didn't have it, you might have to either drastically cut your lifestyle back or go back to work to make up the difference, whether you wanted to or not.

Here is another way to consider how investment loss impacts a retirement portfolio. People do not realize that a 50 percent loss in the stock market destroys a 100 percent gain. Here is an example: You have $100,000 in the market. If it gains 100 percent over the next three years, you will have $200,000. A 50 percent market crash occurs, bringing you back to your original $100,000.

---

9 "S&P 500 Yearly Returns Chart," YCharts.com, https://ycharts.com/indicators/sandp_500_total_return_annual. (May 30, 2017)

If you've been fortunate to have been in the market "at the right time" and made excellent gains, it may be time to consider taking those gains and protecting them from market loss in a fixed indexed annuity with the income rider for retirement income. The income rider guarantees an increasing income account value used to calculate future lifetime income. We'll discuss the ins and outs of fixed indexed annuities and income riders later in this book.

In my years in the business, I've found that these types of investment losses are akin to the most difficult bunker shots. Just like hitting into a sand trap or water hazard can be demoralizing for a golfer, investment loss can be demoralizing for investors. For one thing, investors tend to be much more affected by loss than they are by gain. Known as loss aversion, investors tend to react much more emotionally to loss than they do to gain. So loss can be devastating not only financially but also emotionally. Again, this is another reason why I would hate to have to go to a client or clients and tell them they had lost money.

The Next Bear Market Is around the Corner

Because the nature of the markets is so unpredictable, there is no way to know when the next bear market will strike. The last bear market ended in 2009, and the current bull market is the third longest bull market in history.[10] It might even by over by the time this book is printed or by the time you read it; there is no way to know.

What we do know is that the bear will eventually make his presence known. After the two most recent stock market peaks in 1999 and 2007, a 60 percent loss followed[11] those gains when the bear inevitably appeared. For those invested in the stock market, that loss really hurt. In fact, depending on exactly what types of stocks you were invested in, the loss could have been more severe or less. But would a 50 percent loss hurt a lot less than a 60 percent loss? Probably not, because you would still lose a significant amount of wealth. Again, if such losses occur, there was no guarantee that you would ever recover from that loss. If the market did recover, there is no way to know how long that recovery would take. Waiting to find out would likely interrupt your sleep. There is no way to know when you would be able to sleep well at night again.

---

10 "Bull Market Is Third Longest in History," CNN Money, May 6, 2017, http://money.cnn.com/2015/05/06/investing/stocks-market-3rd-longest-us-bull-market/index.html. (June 23, 2017)

11 Stock Market: The Ride (Supplied by Bob).

Investors in other periods and in other situations have lost more. Many of us remember the dot-com bubble in the late 1990s. The technology-heavy NASDAQ stock index experienced heady gains through 1999, when it skyrocketed up by 85.59 percent. Over the next three years, it fell by 39.29 percent, 21.05 percent, and 31.53 percent that brought the index from a high of 4069.31 to a low of 1335.51.[12]

Because the bull market that began in 2009 has lasted so long, it could expire any day. There is no way to know how severe the upcoming bear market will be or how it will impact your investment portfolio. In my opinion, it is a risk that you may not want to take with your savings that is designated for retirement income, especially when there are other options available that will provide reliable, guaranteed income during retirement with the potential to grow your savings on a market risk–free basis.

---

12 "Nasdaq Composite Total Return Index," 1stock1.com, http://www.1stock1.com/1stock1_140. htm. (June 23, 2017)

CHAPTER 6
Make Sure Your Savings Last

There is no doubt that Americans are living longer. An American born in 1900 could expect a lifespan of 47.3 years, while babies born in 2013 can expect to live, on average, to 78.8, according to the US Centers for Disease Control.[13] Life expectancies are increasing due to many factors, including disease prevention, the development of vaccines, medical advancements, improved access to health care, and declining infant mortality.

This is obviously a fortunate development. It gives us the opportunity to accomplish more in our lives and a better chance to see not just our children grow up but also potentially our grandchildren and even great-grandchildren. Enjoying a comfortable retirement is even more important when you are likely to be around for many family events, including baptisms, bar and bat mitzvahs, graduations, and weddings.

That is why financial protection in retirement is important. As we've discussed and will continue to review, accumulating sufficient savings is an important first step, but it isn't the only step. Using the proceeds wisely for reliable, guaranteed income over a potentially long lifespan is just as important. We've discussed how the potential for tragedy creates a need for life and disability insurance. For those who are fortunate enough not to make use of that kind of coverage, it is essential that income in retirement be safeguarded to the greatest extent possible.

While a long life is a gift for many reasons, a long life can also be filled with unexpected events that require a deep pool of savings. For example, health-care

---

13 "Health, United States 2015," U.S. Centers for Disease Control, May 2016, https://www.cdc.gov/nchs/data/hus/hus15.pdf#015. (June 5, 2017)

costs tend to rise in retirement. The Fidelity Investments Retiree Health Care Cost Estimate predicts that a sixty-five-year-old couple who retired in 2016 will spend $260,000 out of pocket to cover health-care costs during their retirement.[14] While retiree spending tends to spike during the first few years of retirement and decline thereafter, facing a long retirement requires sufficient funding so that you have the confidence to enjoy your retirement without worrying about running out of money and being dependent upon others, especially your children.

Older Americans Are Living Longer

As life spans increase, older Americans are living longer, sometimes significantly longer. By 2050, Americans aged sixty-five and over are expected to number 83.7 million, almost double that of its estimated population of 43.1 million in 2014, according to the US Census Bureau.[15] We've mentioned that the average sixty-five-year-old will live into his or her mideighties. A person who turned seventy in 2017 will live longer than that, with women surviving on average to age 87.5 and men until 85.4. For those who are seventy-five in 2017, women are estimated to live on average to 88.6 while men will live on average to 86.9.[16]

Women, generally, live longer than men. In 2014, the latest year for which these statistics are available, life expectancy at birth for women was 81.2 years and 74.6 for men.[17] Because they earn less than men and are more likely to experience periods out of the workforce due to caregiving for children and/or parents, they are more likely to experience financial difficulties in retirement. There is no need for that to occur in families who have sufficient savings and who take care of that savings responsibly through fixed index annuities that provide guaranteed income in retirement.

Scientists believe that there is a point at which life expectancy will not continue to increase, but at this point, we have no idea what that limit might be. It is not unusual for the elderly to achieve their hundredth birthday, and at this point,

---

14 "Health Care Costs for Couples in Retirement Rise to an Estimated $260,000, Fidelity Analysis Shows," Fidelity, August 16, 2016, https://www.fidelity.com/about-fidelity/employer-services/health-care-costs-for-couples-in-retirement-rise. (June 5, 2017)

15 "An Aging Nation: The Older Population in the United States," U.S. Census Bureau, May 2014, https://www.census.gov/prod/2014pubs/p25-1140.pdf.

16 Ibid.

17 U.S. Centers for Disease Control, "Health, United States 2015."

many financial advisors are telling their clients to prepare for a retirement that could last until age ninety-five or one hundred.

Wealthier Americans Live Longer

A recently published Harvard University study[18] revealed that wealthier people live longer than poorer people. Based on 1.4 billion Internal Revenue Service tax records, this study found that life expectancy at age forty varies by more than ten years for women at the top 1 percent of income and women at the bottom 1 percent of income. The wealthiest women typically live to age 88.5, while the poorest women live to 78.5. The wealthiest men close the gap more with women, living to 87.3, while the poorest men live to 72.3, a fifteen-year differential. If the average high-net worth person lives until their late eighties, that means many are living until their nineties.

This is another reason why it makes sense for high-net-worth and ultra-high-net-worth families to plan for a longer retirement. All too often, clients and prospective clients assume they won't live as long as averages predict, and that can lead to mistakes. For example, even when it is not necessary, some people claim social security at age sixty-two. By doing that, their benefit is significantly reduced, especially over a long life. Social security is like an inflation-protected annuity, and it is a shame to deprive yourself of this income, especially if you don't really need it to pay your expenses in early retirement, which most of my clients don't.

As people age in retirement, their needs change. For example, many younger retirees stay in their family home, but as they age, especially into their late seventies and eighties, their needs change. More and more are considering continuing-care communities, where they can access independent-living, assisted-living, and nursing-home care in one facility. Entry into those living situations can be expensive, which is why you need as much guaranteed monthly income as you can acquire.

Implications of Longer Retirements

Think about the implications of a thirty- or thirty-five-year retirement for a few minutes. A longer retirement potentially gives you time to pursue your hobbies

18 "For Life Expectancy, Money Matters," Harvard University, Harvard Gazette, April 11, 2016, http://news.harvard.edu/gazette/story/2016/04/for-life-expectancy-money-matters/.

in more depth; travel; and spend time with your children, grandchildren, great-grandchildren, and friends. It sounds wonderful, especially if you are fortunate enough to experience good health and an active life. Of course, as I have mentioned, it also requires a certain amount of financial support. Many of my clients find that a combination of social security, guaranteed annuity income, and either investment income or pension income generates a sufficient income per month in retirement to maintain their lifestyles.

Many retirees have the potential to achieve that type of income, but it isn't necessarily consistent. Investing in bonds or stocks has the potential to create income, but that income is likely to vary over time, and when you are making travel plans or deciding whether to renovate your home or move, you don't want a stock market downturn or an increase in interest rates to derail your plans.

As lifespans lengthen, it's even more important to proactively manage risk. You have no control over how long you live. But you can control how much you save before retirement and how you manage your savings before and during retirement. Contributing to products such as fixed index annuities can provide you with some certainty amid uncertainty—providing income for life.

CHAPTER 7
Inflation and Spending in Retirement

nflation is the tendency of prices to rise over time. When prices rise, your savings are worth less. That is why you must consider inflation when saving for retirement and spending from a retirement portfolio. Even when inflation is relatively low—as it has been recently—it eats into your savings over time, especially over a long retirement, when you aren't contributing money from a job to support your lifestyle.

Just like the stock market, it is very difficult, if not impossible, to predict the rate of inflation in the future. As many of us will remember, the period from the mid-1960s to the early 1980s was a time of rapidly rising inflation.[19] In fact, inflation rose to nearly 15 percent a year at the end of the 1970s.[20] Since then, inflation has calmed down, averaging 1.76 percent during the past ten years.[21] Since World War II, Inflation has averaged 3.77 percent[22] a year.

In this chapter, we'll consider the factors that contribute to inflation in general and during retirement and how those factors are likely to play out in retirement. While people tend to regard retirement as a monolithic event, it comprises distinct phases with distinct spending patterns within those phases. It's important to

---

19 "The Great Inflation," The Federal Reserve Bank of Atlanta, November 22, 2013, https://www. federalreservehistory.org/essays/great_inflation. (May 15, 2017)

20 Ibid.

21 "Consumer Price Index," U.S. Department of Labor Bureau of Labor Statistics, https://data.bls. gov/pdq/SurveyOutputServlet?request_action=wh&graph_name=CU_cpibrief. (May 15, 2017)

22 Jill Mislinski, "A Long-Term Look at Inflation," Advisor Perspectives, July 15, 2017, https://www. advisorperspectives.com/dshort/updates/2017/06/15/a-long-term-look-at-inflation. (May 15, 2017)

keep all this in mind when considering your retirement assets and how that will translate into monthly income once you actually retire.

Inflation ABCs

The Department of Labor's Bureau of Labor Statistics identifies eight categories of expenses that are used to calculate changes in inflation:

- Food and beverage
- Housing
- Apparel
- Transportation
- Medical care
- Recreation
- Education and communication
- Other goods and services

Housing receives the largest weight in calculations, followed by transportation, food and beverage, and medical care.

Inflation is important because of its impact on spending and savings. When inflation is low, prices rise slowly, and you get more bang for your buck. On the other hand, when inflation is high, prices climb rapidly, and your spending power dissipates more rapidly. Inflation usually stays in a relatively narrow band in developed countries with stable economies.

However, unexpected events such as the oil shocks of the 1970s can spark unexpectedly high inflation. Economies can also get trapped into deflation, a situation in which prices fall over a long period of time. Japan has experienced just such a scenario for years, which has made it difficult for the economy to generate much growth.

When designing a spending plan for retirement that hinges on your ongoing monthly income, inflation is an important component. You don't want to be in a situation where inflation stays high or higher than your expectations for a number of years, because that could compromise your lifestyle. This is another reason why purchasing a fixed annuity may be a good idea because it provides guaranteed monthly income.

Preretirement Spending

Spending patterns during your career tend to follow a predictable trajectory. Most people save for similar long-term goals, including buying a house, paying for children's college education, and, of course, saving for retirement. Vehicle and apparel expenses may be on the high side, especially if you have a long commute and maintain a professional, up-to-date wardrobe. If you are covered by employer-sponsored health insurance, those expenses should be fairly stable, although they may fluctuate depending on the health status of you and your family.

As you move closer to retirement, it is a good idea to track your spending if you aren't doing it already. Getting a handle on your current spending patterns will be helpful in predicting the amount of income you will need in retirement, although some components of your spending will likely change. Track your bills and expenses for three to four months to make sure that you are capturing a reliable sample. This is easily accomplished through many smartphone apps, some of which allow you to scan receipts directly into your phone or download your online banking records.

Retirement Spending

The facts about aggregate retirement spending—actual spending trends by retired individuals and couples—are backed by some interesting research. One study found that retirees tend to initially spend less than when they were working, see their spending drop further as they move into their seventies, and then gradually rise, only exceeding preretirement thresholds into their nineties.[23] A J.P. Morgan Asset Management study[24] into the changes in spending experienced by retirees observed that retirees reduce spending in apparel, services, transportation, and mortgage payments. Increased spending is observed on health care through the midseventies and into the mideighties and beyond. That makes sense, as retirees can cut back on clothing and commuting expenses immediately upon retirement.

23 David Blanchard, "Exploring the Retirement Consumption Puzzle," *The Journal of Financial Planning* 27, no. 5 (2014): 34–42. https://www.onefpa.org/journal/Pages/MAY14-Exploring-the-Retirement-Consumption-Puzzle-.aspx. (May 25, 2017)

24 Katherine Roy and Sharon Carson, "Retirement Insights: Spending in Retirement," J.P. Morgan Asset Management, August 2014, https://am.jpmorgan.com/blob-gim/1383280121551/83456/RI_Spending_in_retirement.pdf. (May 25, 2017)

This study noted five distinct spending personas, each with their own specific spending patterns and behaviors. The most common personas are foodies and homebodies, who spend more on food, beverages, and big box store purchases and mortgages, home renovations, and furnishings, respectively. A smaller percentage of retirees spend significant amounts of money on travel and health care. Understanding where you fit into that dynamic can help predict spending in retirement, which, in turn, helps align spending with the income available.

Another approach to understanding retirement spending patterns revolves around how spending goes through distinct phases as we age. Early in retirement, your lifestyle doesn't change that much, except for the fact that the time you spent at work is spent engaging in other activities. As you move into the mid- and late seventies, your activity level decreases, and you spend more time at home, tapering down on traveling. Finally, as you move into your mid- to late eighties and beyond, health concerns take over.

Several research studies have found that spending drops consistently as you age through retirement.[25] As I noted above, spending doesn't just decline—what you spend on changes. While health-care spending does increase later in retirement, that spending is offset by reductions in other types of spending.

Incorporating some of these ideas into your retirement spending and income plan will help give it some structure and context. Of course, each individual situation is unique. Anyone's retirement budget can be wrecked by a prolonged stay in a nursing home at any point in retirement. You might want to travel more or purchase a vacation home in retirement, which could push your travel and leisure expenses beyond the averages.

I work closely with my clients to figure out a retirement-income plan that matches their expenses. There is nothing more important than having enough income to prosper and enjoy retirement, no matter how long it lasts. That is the essence of the SWAN—sleep well at night—principle.

---

25 Michael Kitces, "Using Age Banding to Estimate How Spending Will Decline in Retirement," Nerd's Eye View Blog, November 2, 2016, https://www.kitces.com/blog/age-banding-by-basu-to-model-retirement-spending-needs-by-category/. (May 25, 2017)

Impact of Inflation

Obviously, you have to plan on prices going up during your retirement, which will gradually erode your spending power, especially over two or three decades. We all know that $1 in 1960 went much further than $1 in 2017. So an $8,000 or $9,000 a month income, composed of social security, an annuity, and a pension income or other investment income, must include the potential to offset future inflation.

Here are a couple of examples of how inflation erodes purchasing power over time, using $10,000 as a base amount. To have the same purchasing power you did in 2007 with $10,000, you would need $11,909 in 2017. To have the same purchasing power you did in 1997 with $10,000, you would need $15,310 in 2017. Finally, to have that same $10,000 in purchasing power in 1987 you would need $21,914 in 2017, more than double.[26]

If your monthly income doesn't increase to offset the impact of inflation, you will either have to reduce your spending or find another source of income. It isn't always easy to find another source of income in retirement, so reducing spending may be the most likely option. This isn't something that you should have to do. One of the major reasons why I like deferred annuities so much is they offer growth potential while deferred so that when it comes time to take income, you may not have to possibly cut back on your lifestyle. With fixed annuities, you are in the driver's seat, set to enjoy guaranteed income for life.

How to Manage Inflation

Let's take a look at the potential of the various components of your monthly income to keep up with inflation:

- **Social Security**: Fortunately, social security may automatically make cost of living adjustments (known as COLA) to increase the size of a monthly benefit to keep pace with inflation.
- **Deferred Annuities**: The deferred fixed annuities offer the potential growth that can help offset the effects of inflation until receiving income.

26 "CPI Inflation Calculator," US Bureau of Labor Statistics, https://data.bls.gov/cgi-bin/cpicalc.pl. (May 25, 2017)

- **Defined Benefit Pensions**: Many defined benefit pensions may feature some type of cost of living adjustment. It depends on the plan on how much that will be, if any.
- **Investments**: This depends on what type of investments you have. Investments in the stock market have the ability to increase in value more than inflation, but can also decline in value. CDs pay out regular guaranteed interest, but whether they keep up with inflation depends on their interest rate.

CHAPTER 8
Avoid Retirement Risks

n the first section of this book, we've spent a lot of time talking about how to protect your family from all the potential retirement risks. These risks are no joke—and you can't rely on your intelligence to avoid them. It didn't matter how smart the millions of investors were who got hurt in the crash of 1987, the dot-com disaster of 2000, and the financial crisis of 2007–08. No—everyone went down together. And some who went down never came back up. You may not be comfortable subjecting your family to market risk—you can take steps to protect the wealth that you have worked so hard to create.

In a similar fashion, you can't predict how the market will perform or how long you will live. None of us has a crystal ball, and we all face a degree of uncertainty about any one of these risks individually or all of them together:

- Market risk: the risk that your investments won't perform as expected
- Longevity risk: the risk that you and your spouse will outlive your savings
- Inflation risk: the risk that inflation will erode the value of your savings

There are many related risks, but these are the major ones. Retirement used to be simple—when social security first began paying benefits in 1940, life expectancy was much shorter. In the decades since, the rise and fall of the corporate pension has created more exposure to the risks of retirement for baby boomers and the millennials who come after them. There were decades in the fifties, sixties, seventies, and even into the eighties and nineties, where many could count on not only a corporate pension but also corporate health care that supplemented Medicare. For many families, that is no longer the case. They must navigate the risks of retirement on their own. Utilizing an instrument that creates guaranteed, reliable income, potentially for life, may be the best answer to many of the problems and risks that retirement poses.

Correlations

Typically, the word correlation is used to refer to investments that perform in a similar way in similar situations. Most investment professionals help families construct a diversified portfolio to avoid a portfolio where the assets are likely to perform in the same way. However, there are unusual situations, like the most recent financial crisis, where previously uncorrelated assets perform in the same way.[27] In that situation, many investment assets took a big hit, because there was so much fear in the markets that investors sold anything that wasn't seen as exceptionally safe, like US Treasuries.

The term can also refer to other types of factors, such as the risks that we've discussed. For example, many retirees might be able to handle any one of those three risks, even if they weren't completely prepared for them. However, what can happen, just like in a financial crisis, is that two or three of these risks can occur at once, meaning that anyone who isn't well prepared could experience a devastating impact on their retirement savings.

We've looked at the potential cost of market declines from the lens of the 38.5 percent decline in the S&P 500 in 2007.[28] What about if that was just the start of a bear market that lasted for a decade? Could your savings, if invested in the stock market during retirement, withstand that sort of battering?

What if your beloved spouse developed a chronic illness and needed significant help to stay at home or was forced by medical circumstances into a nursing home? That could cost anywhere from $62,000 to $124,000 a year, depending on the type of care needed and where you live, based on 2026 costs calculated by Genworth.[29] As we've discussed, medical expenses are climbing, and you can expect them to at

27 Nir Kaissar, "A Risky Assumption Lurks in Your Portfolio," Bloomberg, September 16, 2016, https://www.bloomberg.com/gadfly/articles/2016-09-16/portfolio-risk-asset-correlation-happens-when-you-need-it-least. (June 15, 2017)

28 CNN Money, "Stock Losses This Year Were Broad based and Dramatic." (June 18, 2017)

29 "Compare Long Term Care Costs Across the United States (Based on the 2016 Cost of Care Survey)," Genworth, https://www.genworth.com/about-us/industry-expertise/cost-of-care.html. (June 17, 2018)

least cost you what Fidelity estimates, which is $275,000 for a couple throughout retirement, but there is no guarantee that your costs won't be higher.[30] Medical inflation could spike, or you could experience a situation like the one described above or something like a type of rare cancer where treatments might be available, but they might not be covered by Medicare or other insurance. In that case, your retirement savings would need to be stretched to cover life-saving treatments.

What if inflation spiked, severely eroding the value of your assets at the same time you experienced a serious, adverse medical event? These situations are, unfortunately, well within the realm of possibility. We all have friends and relatives who have been struck by untimely illness and who have not only struggled with the treatments involved and their side effects but also with the expenses associated with those treatments.

Or what if all three happened at the worst possible time—a run of inflation and market declines just as a person was celebrating his or her ninety-fifth birthday? What effect could this have on his or her retirement savings? Could it weather such a perfect storm of events?

If not, you've got a problem. We all hope that not even one of these events will happen, let alone all of them. But you must plan for the worst and hope for the best. Otherwise, you and your family may be exposed to too much chance and risk. You can't turn a blind eye to the risks out there and hope that you get lucky. As they say, you need to make your own luck. The way to do that with retirement planning is to contribute to products that provide reliable, guaranteed income over a lifetime, such as fixed index annuities.

The Decision

Choice is powerful. As the illustrations above reveal, every choice has a consequence. It may not be one we expect, and it may not come at the right time. As you consider what to do with your hard-earned retirement savings, don't forget that the consequence of not choosing wisely or well could be exposing yourself and your family to a retirement where you can't enjoy the activities that you want and where you aren't sleeping well at night.

---

30 "Health Care Costs for Couples in Retirement Rise to an Estimated $275,000, Fidelity Analysis Shows," Fidelity Investments, August 24, 2017, https://www.fidelity.com/about-fidelity/employer-services/health-care-costs-for-retirees-rise. (June 18, 2017)

What is the key to choosing wisely? Weighing the risks that we've discussed in the first part of this book. With these risks in mind, it makes sense to at least allocate part of your retirement savings to a fixed index annuity that will provide reliable, guaranteed income. When your income is guaranteed to drop into your bank account every month, you can relax, knowing that your expenses are covered. As I've shown in the first part of this book, you have to have a plan. Without a plan, you may just drift into retirement with the investments and savings that you have right now, which may or may not be suitable.

For anyone interested in a reliable, guaranteed stream of income throughout retirement, that plan may include fixed index annuities. These products position you for a retirement that is free of worry about outliving income, leaving time for all the activities you want to enjoy—time with your family, travel, hobbies, and volunteer work. It's hard to focus on those if you are concerned about whether you will have enough money to cover your expenses on a month-to-month basis. Purchasing a fixed index annuity can help you and your spouse sleep well at night not worrying about retirement income—a perfect illustration of the SWAN principle.

CHAPTER 9
The Fact Finder

The Fact Finder is a tool I use with new clients and with clients who are transitioning to a new stage of life, including retirement. It's important to assess what you own (assets) and what you owe (liabilities) as well as your income and expenses so you have a better idea of your current financial position. In addition, I use the Fact Finder to determine what your current savings and investments are, which reveals whether you are well positioned for retirement based on your risk tolerance.

As I have repeatedly noted, I am not a fan of risk. I tend to attract clients who have a similar philosophy—men and women who prefer stability and protection over the potential for a bigger gain (and also the potential for a bigger loss, because you can't have one without the other). If you're reading this book, it's likely that you also have a preference for guarantees over risk.

In this chapter, the last chapter of the first section, we'll go over the various components of the Fact Finder as well as what I look for in terms of matching retirement income with expenses so that you will have the opportunity to experience the retirement of your dreams through the reliable, guaranteed income that fixed index annuities can provide.

Assets and Liabilities

Your assets are what you own and your liabilities are what you owe. This includes your house, your cars, any student loans, and credit-card debt. You may also have other types of assets such as a boat or vacation home or collectibles. In the early part of a career, it is likely that your liabilities will exceed your assets, but as you move ahead in your career, that pendulum will start to swing in the other direction. As many of my clients move closer to retirement, that pendulum moves even further in the direction of the assets, as they pay off their mortgage. In many cases, they are in a strong cash position, so they can afford to buy a new car with cash, although it might make sense to borrow when rates are low.

Going into retirement with as little debt as possible is a good idea. That's because debt service—monthly loan payments—can suck up your income, leaving less to live on. While everyone's situation is different, going into retirement debt-free leaves you with a lot of flexibility. A mortgage-free house could be used to qualify for a traditional line of credit that could be used as the basis for an emergency fund, if that is needed at some point.

Your assets can be divided into a number of categories: qualified retirement-savings accounts, savings and investments, liquid assets, and other nonfinancial illiquid assets. Qualified retirement-savings assets include 401(k)-type company-sponsored retirement accounts as well as 457 plans, profit-sharing plans, and IRA accounts as well as traditional pension plans that are specifically designed to provide for your income during retirement. Other types of savings and investments can include bank accounts, insurance policies, annuity contracts, mutual funds, stocks, other investments, or other special types of accounts, such as college savings accounts for your children or grandchildren. Of those other types of financial assets, liquid assets are made up of financial assets that can easily be turned into cash with little or no fee to do so, such as CDs, checking accounts, savings accounts, and money-market accounts. Illiquid, nonfinancial assets are assets that can't be quickly sold for cash, such as your home, a boat, or collectibles. I'm most concerned about liquid assets and retirement accounts, because those are the basis for generating retirement income.

Income and Expenses

Once you retire, you will likely be living on the monthly income generated from any contributions you make to a fixed index annuity, as well as social security, a pension if you have one, and investment income. Understanding the components of your retirement income and where your monthly income will come from is very important.

It's easy to see what your social-security income will be in retirement—social security provides a yearly statement to all beneficiaries. If you establish an account with www.socialsecurity.gov, you can check into that website any time and find out what your benefit would be at various retirement ages. The earliest age that you can take social security is sixty-two, currently. If you wait, your benefit will continue to grow until age seventy. Your full retirement age depends on the year you were born. Spouses can claim at different ages to maximize their income through retirement. The longer you wait to claim, the larger your monthly benefit will be. Many people underestimate their lifespan and claim early, before their full retirement age, which means a lower monthly benefit. Because you will continue to receive social security throughout your life, it can make sense to wait because a larger monthly benefit can pay off as you get older. No matter how long you live, you will continue to receive social security and any social-security cost-of-living adjustments.

Investment income can encompass many types of income. Some of my clients have rental properties from which they receive monthly income, which is a type of investment income. You may also decide to maintain some investments in the stock or bond markets, which generate dividends and interest, which could be another source of investment income. If you have certificates of deposit, they also fall under the category of investment income.

Some retirees, such as teachers and other government workers, are fortunate enough to have pensions. Pensions vest over a number of years, and once you have a certain number of years of service, you are eligible to take a pension. Then, if you contribute to a fixed index annuity, you will gain another stream of monthly income once you decide to begin taking monthly payments.

We've discussed what average monthly expenses are for most people during their working years and in retirement. In the Fact Finder, we will discuss your specific spending patterns to determine how much of your expenses will carry over to retirement and what expenses you may add to enjoy that retirement.

Analyzing Retirement Investments and Income

One of the most important parts of the Fact Finder is the analysis of your retirement investments and income. Frequently, retirement savings are invested through a 401(k)-company-sponsored retirement plans. Those funds are usually invested in the markets, in some type of mutual fund. Fortunately, many companies permit employees, entrepreneurs, or partners to transfer some or all of those funds into IRA accounts. IRAs offer a lot of flexibility, including the ability to purchase a fixed index annuity. You can also use taxable accounts to purchase a fixed index annuity.

My goal with a retirement investment and asset analysis is to assess the level of risk. The perspective switch from someone who is earning a substantial income to someone in retirement is significant. Some risk is acceptable when you can replace funds lost to a market downturn. When you can't, because you are retired, that is a whole different story. That is why I recommend that my clients place as large a percentage of their retirement assets as possible in a fixed annuity. It's for safeguarding that money so it provides guaranteed income in retirement.

Once your assets are correctly positioned to yield the maximum amount of guaranteed income possible, it is fairly easy to determine the retirement-income picture. The only question is typically when exactly you and your spouse plan to retire and when you will need your income. In some cases, spouses don't retire at the same time, meaning that income is still coming in, so at least some retirement income can be delayed, whether that is social security, annuity income, or investment income. In other cases, you may decide to cut back on your work schedule but not completely retire. I want to ensure that whenever you and your spouse do go ahead and fully retire—whether that is age sixty-five or seventy or later, you will have the income you need to fully and confidently enjoy your retirement.

Moving on to the Back Nine

I've spent the first half of this book outlining the case for reliable, guaranteed income. I know so many entrepreneurs, executives, and professionals who have worked incredibly hard to build careers to provide for their families. From my perspective, it doesn't make any sense to save so doggedly, only to put all that at risk by following a risky retirement strategy. It's similar to the way you want to set up your golf game—if you have a great game going on the front nine, you don't want to blow it with a series of double-bogeys on the back nine. No, you want to stay the course and hold steady. Why jeopardize your hard-earned savings in any way when there is an alternative available that can preserve your savings and ensure that you sleep well at night, not worrying about retirement income?

In the next section of the book—the back nine—we'll explore the case for fixed index annuities. You'll learn about their potential for guaranteed lifetime income, the various contribution options, and the ways that this product can keep your principle protected while offering growth potential. This product completely protects you from downside market risk. When you contribute to one of these annuities, you can let go of any concern about brutal market declines. I love the way that this product offers my clients—and myself and my wife, because we have also contributed large sums of money to these products—the potential for growth and protection from a down market. Keep reading the rest of the book for even more information about all the wonderful features and benefits of these products that can help you realize the SWAN principle—sleep well at night.

Section 2
The Back Nine

CHAPTER 10
Your Financial Bridge

As you move closer to retirement, preparing your finances to cross the bridge into actual retirement is of paramount importance. There are many aspects to creating a stable, confident retirement, but the most important, as we have discussed, is ensuring you have a reliable income stream to cover your retirement expenses.

For most people, real concern around retirement finances tends to rise as they move into their mid and late fifties. Many have saved throughout their careers, especially my current and prospective clients who are successful professionals, entrepreneurs, and executives. But you may not have a solid handle on exactly how much retirement savings you have, where it is, how it is deployed, and whether it is enough to see you through a potential thirty- or thirty-five-year-long retirement.

In addition, the risk aspect of the risk-reward relationship is of more concern to you than the reward. If you've diligently saved and invested over your career, you've reaped the rewards that the market has to offer. With retirement looming, now is the time to lock those gains in and turn to the work involved in preserving and protecting your assets.

In this chapter, we'll go over some of the steps you can take to prepare yourself financially to cross the bridge into retirement. Then, in the rest of this section, we'll explore in detail how fixed index annuities can provide guaranteed income in retirement, providing the financial freedom and flexibility so you can sleep well at night.

Getting to the Bridge

You can't make it successfully to the bridge if you haven't protected yourself earlier during the height of your career. While we all hope for an uninterrupted progression through our careers, that doesn't always happen. My son-in-law is a perfect example. He is a successful chiropractor in Texas with a growing practice that he runs with the help of an associate. Several years ago, he was diagnosed with an injury to his wrist, which made it impossible for him to treat patients. Because of the personal and business disability policies I had set him up with earlier in his career, he was able to continue to support himself and his family as well as pay the business expenses associated with his practice while his associate continued to treat patients.

Fortunately, he recovered from his injury and is back to running his practice, so he stopped the disability payments. This is a great example of how protection such as life and disability insurance can keep a retirement plan on track. Without personal or business disability insurance, entrepreneurs are heavily exposed to financial loss in the event of an injury that doesn't permit them to engage in their business. In fact, the lack of such coverage could result in financial catastrophe and even bankruptcy. When you're covered, your retirement funds can continue to grow and you may even be able to continue to contribute to them.

Your Resources

If you're like many people, you may have worked for different employers throughout the course of your career and could have contributed to several company-sponsored retirement plans. Those plans may be held by different custodians, and you may receive so many different statements that you don't have a complete picture of what exactly you've saved for retirement. If you are married, you could easily have five or even ten different company-sponsored retirement accounts with different companies.

Hopefully, you either have a financial professional whom you are working with and who already has a handle on this aspect of your finances or you use an app or site that offers portfolio consolidation so you can receive a holistic view of all your retirement assets and understand how much you have invested and where that money is currently invested.

Some professionals prefer to consolidate their retirement resources as much as possible, while others prefer to work with several financial professionals who can help them manage different aspects of their financial lives. Whichever approach you prefer is up to you; just make sure that you have a full understanding of how much you have saved, where it is maintained and how it is invested.

Transitioning

Many of my clients are in the process of transitioning from their full-on career mode to the preretirement phase. This involves getting all of their financial ducks in a row so that they are fully prepared to make the move to retirement whenever they are ready. Through the "bridge" years as I call them, I stay in close touch, ensuring that all their financial questions related to our financial, insurance, and annuity relationships are answered and that they know exactly where they stand.

I'm a fanatic about customer service and customer relationships and am proud to call many of my clients my friends. Not a year goes by without me contacting every single one of my clients, usually several times a year if not more often, by letter, by phone, and if they are nearby, in person. If you have a financial advisor or agent from whom you haven't heard in years, you might want to rethink that relationship.

My clients know that I am here for them anytime and anywhere. As I have mentioned, many of them purchased life insurance and disability from me when they were young professionals, and I have stayed in touch. Many are now calling on me to help them with their retirement-income concerns. After consulting with me and learning about the benefits of deferred index annuities, many have contributed some of their retirement savings into annuities. This forward-looking decision helps ensure that they will make it to the other side of the bridge, and beyond, without anxiety or worry about the future.

How It Works

As I have noted, there are multiple ways to purchase a fixed index annuity. I have a client whom I initially met when he was a medical student. He purchased life insurance and disability, which he fortunately hasn't had to use. He is now in his midfifties and is getting more and more concerned about the stock market and a potential downturn or a decline in the value of the money he has saved in his retirement plan. A portion of his retirement savings is tied up in profit-sharing plans. In some cases, professionals can move funds out of a profit-sharing plan into an IRA so that they can purchase a fixed annuity. In this case, he was able to, and he placed a sum of money in the fixed index annuity. This move relieved his anxiety about the market and having assets overexposed to the risk the stock market poses. He doesn't plan to touch that for more than ten years. In that time, it has the potential to grow so that when he is ready to retire, there will be a monthly stream of income that he can count on, guaranteed for the rest of his life. He may add more to this account or purchase another fixed index annuity once he has more funds available, ultimately increasing his lifelong monthly income.

Many of my clients have worked hard enough their entire lives that they have disposable income in a taxable account that they could use to purchase a fixed annuity. For example, an entrepreneur who sells a business prior to retirement usually has a significant amount of cash available from the proceeds of that business. Placing a significant amount of funds into an annuity that then grows before it is utilized during retirement could provide an additional amount of income in retirement.

For many, rolling funds from company-sponsored retirement accounts that have accumulated throughout their careers into an IRA may beneficial. Deploying some of those funds into a fixed index annuity sets the stage for retirement-income protection. Obviously, the more money invested, the larger the ongoing amount of income. Some of my clients prefer to place money into one annuity, while others have multiple annuities. Either approach can be effective.

In the case of multiple annuities, these clients have utilized additional funds as the years go by from a variety of sources, including capital gains, an inheritance, a gift, or a change in retirement strategy to purchase annuities. My wife and I own a number of annuities with different features. New products come along, and as I have mentioned before, if it is a product I am going to recommend to a client, it has to be one that I am willing to participate in myself.

I've discovered some newer deferred annuity products through the continuing education that I constantly pursue to keep my knowledge and skills sharp. I am in touch with a variety of annuity providers across the country, and when new products are released, I will review the product in depth before I recommend it to my clients. This review includes the product features, benefits as well as limitations. I will also review the insurer's current financial and strength ratings by independent ratings agencies.

The Back Nine

As you read the second half of this book, you'll learn more about the specific features of fixed index annuities and how they can benefit you and your retirement. We'll walk through some case studies of some of my most successful clients and show how I help clients with planning out their retirement-income needs. Finally, we'll come to the conclusion, with a preview of the financial freedom to sleep well at night when you have a plan for retirement income.

CHAPTER 11
Sources of Reliable Income

Reliable, guaranteed income is the nirvana of retirement. As we've discussed throughout this book, generating a stream of reliable, guaranteed income creates an incredible sense of stability in retirement, allowing you to spend time with the people you love doing the things that you love. Until recently, retirees could just about take reliable, guaranteed income for granted—they didn't have to even think much about their resources in retirement; they would take their pension, social security, and any investments and enjoy the rest of their lives.

However, as corporate retirement plans have moved from defined benefit plans to defined contribution plans, such as 401(k)s, more preretirees are at the mercy of what they have saved and how the markets have performed. At the same time, as interest rates have fallen during the past several decades, it is harder and harder to generate reliable income through investing.[31] Dividend yields are also lower than average.[32] This creates a dilemma for many current retirees and preretirees, who lack access to traditional sources of reliable income.

In this chapter, we'll review retirement-savings vehicles and sources of reliable income and their current status along with options such as fixed index annuities. This product is designed to pick up the slack, providing a reliable, guaranteed income stream needed to prosper during retirement.

---

31 Kimberly Amadeo, "Fed Funds Rate History: Highs, Lows and Chart with Major Events," August 2, 2017, TheBalance.com, https://www.thebalance.com/fed-funds-rate-history-highs-lows-3306135. (July 1, 2017)

32 "S&P 500 Dividend Yield by Year," Multpl.com, http://www.multpl.com/s-p-500-dividend-yield/table. (July 1, 2017)

Bank Products

Because of their federal guarantee, banks, savings, and loans and credit union accounts provide conservative savings options. For many years, retirees and those who wanted to save conservatively used savings accounts, money-market accounts, and certificates of deposit as sources of reliable savings. While you can still certainly save using these vehicles, with low-interest rates the interest won't accumulate as fast as you may desire. With low-interest-rate environments, the interest earned may not keep up with the rising costs of living due to inflation.

That's because rates for even long-term CDs are quite low. A check into Bankrate.com national CD yields revealed that the best rate available for a CD with a $25,000 minimum was 2.35 percent.[33] If you purchased that CD, at the end of that five-year period, you would receive $28,116.93, a whole $3,116.93 more than your original amount. If inflation weighs in at about that rate—which isn't out of the realm of possibility, given historical trends—you would stay even without any gain. Taking inflation into consideration, CDs may not be your first choice in retirement savings. In October 2017, one of the best rates for a one-year CD was 1.65 percent, while the rate for a three-year CD was around 1.8 percent, according to Bankrate.com.[34] Factor in taxes due on the interest if in a nonqualified account (not an IRA) and your net yield is much lower. Again, nothing to write home about.

One reason CD rates are relatively generous compared to the rates of savings, money-market, and checking account is your money is locked up. If you cash out early, there are penalties. Rates for savings accounts depend on the minimum balance—the higher the minimum balance, the higher the rate. In some cases, you can get higher rates with online-only banks. Current rates for savings and money-market accounts range from 0.25 percent to 1.25 percent depending on the amount deposited and the bank.[35] While you won't have to lock your money up to receive these rates in return, they still aren't much. The bottom line is that neither CDs, money-market accounts, nor savings accounts can provide you with the guaranteed income you can't outlive.

---

33 "CD Rates," Bankrate.com, July 22, 2017, www.bankrate.com/partners/sem/cd-rates (July 1, 2017)

34 "CD Rates," Bankrate.com, October 15, 2017, http://www.bankrate.com/cd.aspx. (Oct. 15, 2017)

35 "Savings Account Rates," Bankrate.com, July 22, 2017, http://www.bankrate.com/banking/savings/rates/?ic_id=home_smart%20spending_homepage-compare-rates_savings-checking_savings-money-market. (July 22, 2017)

Dividends

Dividends are usually a cash distribution that companies pay out of their profits. Not all companies pay dividends. For those that do, payments are typically made on a quarterly basis. Many investors rely on stocks that pay dividends for that elusive combination of income and growth. Although the number of companies that are paying dividends is rising, the trailing twelve-month dividend yield for the S&P 500 index in the third quarter of 2016 fell below 2 percent, according to FactSet Research.[36]

We're back in 2 percent area territory. So, folks, dividends aren't the magic answer either. While some dividends are higher than others, just like with other types of investment, there is usually a risk–reward relationship. In other words, the more reliable the investment and lower the risk, the lower the dividend. The higher the risk, the higher the dividend. If you're like me—which you probably are, because you are reading this book—you don't like risk. That means you may want to avoid anything that increases your risk, including chasing yield.

Yields have a lot to do with the overall economy. The Federal Reserve cut interest rates to near zero nine years ago to stimulate the economy during the Great Recession.[37] Low rates are great for borrowers, which was one of the reasons for the rate cuts—to stimulate businesses and consumers to make investments in big ticket items. But for savers, these low rates can be a disaster, because you may not be able to count on income generated through traditional CDs, dividend stocks, and other sources to get you through retirement. While the Fed is raising rates, they are doing it slowly, and the increases are filtering back to deposit products even more slowly.

Pensions

As we've discussed, for most employees, the defined benefit plans are going the way of the dinosaur. The few private employers with defined benefit plans are eliminating them in favor of defined contribution plans such as 401(k) plans. From the employee perspective, the major benefit of a defined benefit plan is

---

36 "Dividend Quarterly," FactSet Research, December 20, 2016, https://insight.factset.com/hubfs/Dividend%20Quarterly/Dividend%20Quarterly%20Q3%202016_12.20.pdf. (July 22, 2017)

37 Jon Hilsenrath, "Fed Cuts Rates Near Zero to Battle Slump," *Wall Street Journal*, December 17, 2008, https://www.wsj.com/articles/SB122945283457211111. (July 22, 2017)

that the responsibility of making payments to retirees and ensuring solvency is on the company providing the pension plan rather than the individual retiree. Although many companies contribute to their employees' 401(k) plans, it is the responsibility of the individual employee to manage their own contributions by deciding upon investments offered in the plan. And when you're talking about investments, you are back to assuming more risks.

All that may be fine when you are younger—in your thirties and forties, there is still plenty of time to ride out the ups and downs of the markets. There is also time to continue to contribute. Typically, contributions grow as you age, because your salary goes up and you understand why it is important to save for retirement. However, by the time you are in your fifties and heading toward your sixties, you don't necessarily want stock market risk to rain on your retirement parade. You may want reliability and protection. In other words, you want to sleep well at night, not worrying about your retirement income before and during your retirement.

Fixed Index Annuities

This brings us to the fixed index annuity, which I believe may be a suitable option for those of us who want reliable and guaranteed income with the potential for growth. In the next three chapters, we will explore how this product works and how fixed index annuities can provide you with ongoing monthly income that you can count on, regardless of how long your retirement lasts. If you are married, the fixed index annuity may also provide for your spouse if you pass away first. Basically, this is a one-stop destination for retirement income. Deferred annuities grow during the late stages of your working career and in the early stages of your retirement; particularly, if you elect an optional lifetime income rider, then they can pay a lifetime income (if this option is selected) once you elect to begin receiving monthly income payments. I love them—they are a real win-win retirement-savings and income product.

CHAPTER 12

Your Ticket to Retirement-Income Stability: The Fixed Index Annuity

As many of my clients move toward retirement, I have found that fixed index annuities are one of the most useful products I can recommend. June 2017 marked the beginning of my forty-seventh year in the insurance and annuity industries, and during that time, I have worked with many clients and evaluated many products. For professionals, entrepreneurs, and executives who are concerned about the protection of their savings during retirement, the fixed index annuity is very valuable for future retirement-income planning.

Many of my clients have saved for retirement for years using IRAs, 401(k) plans, pension, and profit sharing to fund their retirement income. In my opinion, the best way to contribute a lump sum of money for retirement in the future is to use a fixed index annuity. Individuals who have large sums of money in the stock market, bank CDs, money-market funds, and other types of investments should also consider a fixed index annuity. You can own a fixed index annuity either within an IRA or outside of an IRA. If you participate outside of a retirement account, those funds could come from cash you have in the bank, a bonus from work, or taxable investments that might currently be invested in the market or in a certificate of deposit. I love how flexible these products are, offering many benefits that I will detail below.

Unlike some insurance and financial professionals, I put my money where my mouth is. My wife and I have 96 percent of our IRA funds and 98 percent of all personal funds in annuities of which approximately 97 percent is in fixed index annuities and 3 percent in fixed annuities. We own twelve index and three traditional fixed annuities for the same reason I recommend these products. I want more reliable options for my future. As I have emphasized, annuities provide reliable guaranteed income versus the market risk using stocks. Hence, the SWAN concept—sleep well at night.

Avoiding Risk

At this point, I'm sure you have realized that I really dislike risk. While many people are drawn to the stock market and other risky investments when they are younger and have many more years to work, I have seen how my clients and many others in the fifties and sixties become less and less comfortable taking risks over time. That makes perfect sense. When you are younger, time is on your side—you have time to ride out the ups and downs of the market when you are young, say in your twenties and thirties and even in your forties. However, as your retirement and savings balances grow bigger and you get closer to retirement, the stakes get higher and higher. You get to the point in your career and in your life where a significant setback in the market could exact too high a price.

Imagine working hard your whole life to amass savings of $2 million for retirement. That may be, for most people, plenty of money to provide retirement protection, even through a thirty- or thirty-five-year retirement. However, if you retired at the end of 2007 with that amount invested in the S&P 500, your $2 million would be worth $1.23 million.[38] That could be a scary situation when you are close to or in retirement. You would need to consider options that include scaling back your standard of living, take more risks, or go back to work to be sure that you could make it through your retirement.

Downside Protection

We've discussed previously how volatility can wreak havoc on the most carefully planned retirement. Volatility can result in negative returns, positive returns, or flat returns over a period of time. The advantage of purchasing a fixed index annuity is that the value won't decrease. In fact, the value may increase due to the crediting of interest. Those credits would be locked in at the end of the crediting period—not subject to future downturns in the market.

---

38 CNN Money, "Stock Losses This Year Were Broad based and Dramatic." (July 22, 2017)

One of my favorite features of fixed index annuities is the downside protection against losses due to a market downturn. What this means is if the index goes down, you do not lose any of your premium. Not only that, but you would also still retain any interest previously credited in years that the index performed positively.

Specifically, what this means is that if you participate in a fixed index annuity that uses the S&P 500 index as a benchmark, and the S&P 500 index falls in any given year, the annuity value remains the same as it was at the beginning of the crediting period. In other words, the account won't experience any loss due to the decrease in the index. No matter how much the S&P 500 would go down—5 percent or 50 percent—your annuity value doesn't decrease.

If the S&P 500 index increases, the annuity will have interest credits based on the percentage of gain. The interest credits won't be the same as the increase in the index but will be based on the calculation method used in the specific annuity contract. For example, if the S&P 500 goes up 10 percent in one year, you might be credited with 4 percent based on the specific strategy that you chose in the contract. In other words, you share in the upside potential of the market without experiencing any downside risks.

Volatility Protection

Market volatility can be financially and emotionally distressing. Since investing in the stock market through individual stocks, mutual funds, or ETFs offers no guarantee, your investment could fall in value at any time by any amount. You can't count on how much principal you will have in the future or how much income that might produce on a monthly basis. Many experts say that the insecurity retirees experience as a result leads them to underspend, which means they skip on trips, hobbies, activities, and other things that they had planned on enjoying during retirement.[39]

For example, if you invested $100,000 in the S&P 500 through a mutual fund or exchange-traded fund and the index fell by 40 percent that year, your savings

---

39 Meir Statman, "The Mental Mistakes We Make with Retirement Spending," *Wall Street Journal*, April 24, 2017, https://www.wsj.com/articles/the-mental-mistakes-we-make-with-retirement-spending-1492999921. (July 22, 2017)

would be worth $60,000. To get back to a $100,000 balance, you would have to gain nearly 67 percent, which could take years.[40]

However, if a fixed index annuity was purchased instead, there would be no loss because the annuity value was due to a decrease in the S&P 500. This is a very important feature with incredible value not only for your confidence in retirement income but also for the stability of your retirement income over time. If you know that your premium will not decline and that it might increase, you can withdraw a specific amount of money each month with confidence. That allows you to pursue all the enjoyable activities you planned on before you retired. Whether it is travel, more time with your family, or hobbies—or all of the above—you can pursue those activities with enjoyment and without worrying that the bottom might fall out of your savings.

Protection of Principal

One of the most significant benefits of fixed index annuities is that your premium remains protected and not subject to downturns in the stock market. Guarantees provided in the annuity contract are backed by the insurance companies. Insurance companies employ many financial professionals with advanced degrees and decades of experience to manage their investment portfolios.

Tax Deferral

If you decide to purchase a fixed annuity with money outside of your qualified retirement accounts, any interest credited is not taxed until the time it's withdrawn from the contract. Qualified retirement accounts such as IRAs, 401(k)s, 403(b)s, SEPs, and other types of plans are tax-deferred by nature.

Tax deferral confers powerful benefits, including allowing money you would otherwise pay in taxes to remain tax deferred and the opportunity to earn interest.

Penalty-Free Withdrawals

If you experience an emergency or need money for some other purpose before you are ready to begin withdrawals from a fixed index annuity, many companies

---

40 There is no outside citation for this figure. It is simple math: $100,000 minus $40,000 = $60,000. To get back to $100,000, that $60,000 would have to grow by 67 percent.

allow penalty-free withdrawals between 5 and 10 percent with no surrender-charge penalty. For example, if you placed $500,000 into a fixed index annuity and wanted to withdraw $25,000–50,000 to renovate your kitchen, if your contract allowed, you may be able to withdraw that money without surrender penalty. Keep in mind annuities are designed for long-term savings for retirement, and as such when purchasing an annuity, clients should have sufficient liquid assets outside the annuity. Additionally, if not over fifty-nine and a half at the time of the withdrawal, the IRS may impose a 10 percent tax penalty.

Ongoing Monthly Income

When you retire and are ready to receive income, that income can be paid over a specific number of years or for the rest of your life. A guaranteed lifetime income rider is very appealing because you don't know how long you will live. As we have mentioned in earlier chapters, many affluent Americans are living longer than ever. With a lifetime income rider, you will keep receiving the same monthly income no matter how long you live.

Premium Bonus

Some companies offer premium bonus rates on the amount of your initial premium at the time of issue. The amount of premium bonus varies by annuity contract and by insurer. If you purchase an annuity with $100,000 and the annuity offers a 5 percent bonus, you would have a contract worth $105,000.

In some cases, you can continue to place money in an annuity and receive a bonus in the first year. So if a company offered a 5 percent bonus on a $200,000 contract, you would have $210,000 right away. Then if you placed another $20,000 a few months later, the same 5 percent bonus would apply, adding another $1000.

Beneficiary Benefits

The death benefits paid are dependent on the provisions of the annuity contract. Typically upon the death of the annuitant, the remaining full accumulated value is available to the designated beneficiary without any surrender charges. In some cases, the spouse if named as the primary beneficiary may qualify for continuation of the contract or be able to start receiving a monthly income payout. Children and other nonspouses who can be named as beneficiaries would receive the death benefit at the time of death.

Fees or Expenses

The entire amount of premium you place in the annuity goes to the accumulated value immediately. It is not reduced by sales charges, set-up fees, or commissions. The commission paid to the selling agent is paid by the insurance company and does not reduce the premium placed in the annuity.

Depending on the features and benefits included in the annuity contract, there may be a fee or expense charged to the value on a regular basis throughout the time that you own your annuity. Any fees or charges can also depend on any optional riders chosen.

CHAPTER 13

How Fixed Index Annuities Work in Practice

As an experienced financial advisor, I understand that many potential clients may not understand how annuities work and what happens when different life and retirement situations arise. The purpose of this chapter is to offer an in-depth examination of the nuts and bolts of a typical fixed-index-annuity product. Many of these features my clients have found help them plan for retirement income and increase their confidence in retirement.

Many fixed annuities offer many appealing features, including the following:

- Principal preservation
- Guaranteed income
- Liquidity features
- Tax deferral
- Probate avoidance
- Premium bonus
- Income riders
- Confinement waivers or riders

Annuity contracts also have certain limitations. As previously mentioned, annuities are designed for long-term retirement savings and are designed with that in mind. An annuity contract typically contains certain limitations on how much and/or how often money can be withdrawn from a contract, how interest is calculated and credited, vesting of premium bonuses, and surrender-charge periods.

Principal Preservation

As we've mentioned, a major advantage of purchasing an annuity versus other options is the protection of your principal. Unlike the stock market, where the value of your investment is at risk for loss, an annuity contract guarantee provides that the value of the annuity can't be reduced due to market downturns. You want to consider the financial strength of an insurance company by reviewing the insurance-company ratings by companies such as the A.M. Best and Standard and Poor rating agencies.

Guaranteed Income

While virtually all fixed index annuities offer guaranteed income, payouts can occur in different ways. For example, many annuities offer payouts over ten or twenty years or over a lifetime. Deferred annuities typically remain deferred, allowing for interest accumulation prior to turning on income. The interest credited depends on what type of allocation you select when you purchase the annuity. And as we've mentioned, downside protection ensures that the annuity won't lose value, regardless of what happens to the economy and markets during the deferral period.

Many annuity owners find the lifetime guaranteed-income payout very appealing. A lifetime guaranteed-income payout means just that—no matter how long you live, you will continue to receive guaranteed monthly income from the annuity. Having a product that offers that type of guarantee can seem a bit perplexing, as it isn't easy to understand where the income will come from if you actually outlive your contribution and the interest credited. The insurance company's ability to provide this type of guarantee is called "risk pooling." It's similar to the process the company's financial experts and actuaries follow to develop life-insurance products. The risk of longevity is spread across the entire policyholder pool, allowing actuaries to take into account the life expectancy of many people rather than one.

Because it is more expensive for an insurance company to pay out guaranteed monthly income over a lifetime rather than a set period of time, the amount of income guaranteed for the lifetime payout is less than it would be for a shorter period of time, such as ten or twenty years. That makes sense, because it is more expensive for an insurance company to pay out income over an unknown period of time than a definite, potentially shorter period of time. The fact is, someone who has a lifetime payout could die after fifteen years, which is shorter than some-one who has a twenty-year payout, but because the longevity of a specific per-son is unknown, there are more variables at play in the lifetime income than the twenty-year payout.

Liquidity

Many annuities offer regular access to the principal portion of the accumulated value without penalty. Many products allow contract holders to take out between 5 and 10 percent surrender penalty free each year beginning in the second contract year.

This provides a tremendous amount of flexibility for my clients. For exam-ple, one of my clients whose husband died was the beneficiary of his annuity and elected the spousal assumption death benefit option. Once she was the owner of the annuity, she was able to withdraw a portion of the money to renovate her home without incurring a surrender-charge penalty as the renovation amount was 5 percent of the value of the annuity. She was delighted to free up the cash for this project without having to borrow money or incur a penalty.

If you need more than the free withdrawal provided in the contract, there will be a surrender-charge penalty on the amount over the free-withdrawal percent-age. Annuity surrender charges periods typically that decline over the duration of the surrender-charge period. So the longer you own the annuity, typically the less the penalty becomes over the period.

Tax Deferral

Annuities offer important tax-deferral advantages. When you purchase a fixed index annuity with either qualified or nonqualified money (meaning outside of a qualified retirement account), any interest credited is not taxable until withdrawn from the annuity.

Keep in mind that with nonqualified fixed deferred annuities, the IRS consid-ers any withdrawals from the annuity as interest coming out first and therefore taxable. Once the interest has been distributed, the premium (your previously taxed money) would be considered distributed. In the case of an IRA or other qualified annuity, the entire amount is considered taxable when withdrawn. If you purchase an immediate annuity with nonqualified money, the payments are con-sidered part interest and part premium—the amount of the payment not subject to taxes is referred to as the exclusion ratio. The remaining amount is considered interest and therefore taxable.

For estate-planning purposes, annuities have the ability to bypass the estate and probate processes when an appropriately named beneficiary exists. Your beneficiaries have several options in terms of receiving the proceeds of the annuity—they can either receive the proceeds as monthly income or obtain a lump-sum payment.

Additional-Benefit Rider

Some annuities offer a nursing home or a confinement rider. These riders allow you additional income in the event you become confined or need assistance with daily living activities. Typically these riders have qualification requirements that include not being able to perform, for example, three of the six activities of daily living. For example, if you can't bathe or dress yourself, you could qualify for additional income for a certain amount of time.

This rider is not a substitute for or a type of long-term care insurance, which is a completely different insurance product. Instead, this is a rider that may be available to purchase along with the annuity contract that will provide these benefits as long as you meet the conditions. I highly recommend this feature, if it is available, for the protection it provides as you get older. For many, it helps them stay in their homes and receive care with the ability to pay for it, instead of a nursing or assisted-living facility.

Lifetime Income

Annuities offer a number of options in terms of ongoing monthly income. The deferred annuity contract provides options for periodic income called annuitization. The deferred annuity accumulated value is used to create a stream of income. Once annuitized, the contract no longer holds a lump-sum value, and the stream of income chosen cannot be changed. Upon annuitization, there are fixed periods of time over which you can receive monthly income, typically ten or twenty years. That means, for example, if you start receiving your monthly income benefit at age seventy and you elect a ten-year period to receive income, your monthly income would end at age eighty. After that, your annuity would be terminated, and you would receive no more benefits.

The twenty-year payout is similar. If you started receiving benefits at age seventy, when you turn ninety, those benefits would cease. Lifetime income is also an option to choose from when annuitizing the contract. In addition, you can select a period certain and lifetime income, where income is paid for whichever is longer. For example, life and ten-year certain, which means the income would be paid for your lifetime or ten years, whichever is longer. If death occurs prior to ten years, the beneficiary would receive the remaining payments. In most cases, limited term payments are higher than lifetime income, but you run the risk of outliving the income and having to cut back your lifestyle or to seek help from relatives.

In addition to the annuitization options in an annuity contract, a lifetime income rider may be offered with the annuity contract; the lifetime income rider provides monthly income as long as you live. Even if you live to be one hundred, or older, you will continue to receive the same income. The main difference in annuitization and the lifetime income rider is that the rider provides income without giving up the accumulated value of the contract. The base contract still remains and is able to receive interest credits, and upon death of the annuitant, the death benefit of the remaining value would still be available to the beneficiaries. The lifetime income rider is an optional rider for which a fee is typically charged. I recommend this rider to my clients when income is an objective because it provides so much confidence in your retirement income. Imagine a retirement where you didn't have to worry about outliving your income—what a gift! This is what a lifetime income rider provides. Call it "sleep insurance"—sleep well at night.

Single- and Joint-Payout Options

When you are ready to begin taking monthly benefits from your annuity, you need to decide whether to take a single or joint payout. A joint payout is usually available to legal spouses who are fifty years of age or older. Once you decide what type of payout to take, that decision can't be changed. The benefit in either case—single or joint—depends on your age at the time you begin taking monthly payouts.

Because the joint payout is less than the single payout, I encourage my clients to consider selecting the single payout during their lifetime. Then, once they pass away, many companies allow their surviving spouse to begin monthly payouts based on their own life expectancy and gender. That way, your monthly income is maximized at all times.

CHAPTER 14
Enjoy Lifetime Income

For retirees, there is literally nothing better than a stream of reliable, lifetime-guaranteed income. To know that no matter how long you live and what situations you encounter you will receive income every month provides an incredible sense of protection. This is what helps my clients sleep well at night as they move into retirement.

Without this protection, it is hard to really let go and enjoy your retirement. No matter what is happening—even if you've just shot a ten-under-par golf game—there can be a sense of low-level anxiety in the background. That is because you could be one bear market away from running out of money.

These are the reasons that I frequently recommend annuities with lifetime income benefit riders to my clients. A lifetime income benefit rider provides income throughout your life, and if you name your spouse as primary beneficiary, the benefit may be provided to him or her at death. Should you die first, your spouse may be able to continue the contract under certain circumstances.

There are many factors that influence how much monthly income you will get when you decide to begin taking payments. These include the length of the deferral period, the rate at which your principal has grown, and your age at the time that you begin receiving payments. Below, I'm using a number of examples that are purely for illustration purposes to help you understand the underlying principles by which deferred annuities work.

Impact of Deferred Income

The deferral factor contributes to building a robust stream of income for owners of deferred annuities. By delaying the time period within which you will receive monthly income, you allow your money the opportunity to grow. That means you will potentially receive more income when you finally elect to receive it. A contribution of $100,000 in a twenty-year deferred index annuity with a lifetime income rider will likely experience some growth during that period. That growth will depend on the guaranteed income account interest rate that you elect or the performance of the index and other individual policy factors.

If, for example, that $100,000 grows at a guaranteed rate of 5 percent during that period, you would end up with a principal balance of $271,809.57 by the time you are seventy and you may decide to begin receiving income from the annuity. Clearly your income account has grown, providing you with more monthly income.

Optimal Deferral Period

The optimal deferral period varies depending on individual circumstances. A ten-year period could work well for a couple who purchased a deferred annuity when one partner turned sixty-five. For individuals or couples who purchased a deferred annuity at age fifty, a twenty-year period might work better.

Determining the specific deferral period depends on a number of factors, including the following:

- The age at which you plan to retire
- When you plan to claim social-security benefits
- What other financial resources you have and the income they will provide
- Your health

When my clients purchase deferred annuities, we spend a lot of time discussing their options and making a decision about the length of the deferral period. Obviously, the longer the deferral period is, the greater the eventual amount of income can be. However, the deferral period needs to be carefully considered based on your overall situation.

If you select a ten-year deferral period, your contribution will compound during that period of time, but compounding ceases at the end of the period. That means if you don't begin to take payments until year eleven, twelve, thirteen, or later, your principal won't increase. With the twenty-year deferral period, your principal will grow throughout those two decades, and you can usually start your lifetime income after the eleventh year if desired. However, many contracts provide the option of taking penalty-free withdrawals of up to 5–10 percent of your principal, which you could use if you needed some cash during that period without starting the lifetime income option.

Income-Rider Rate

The income rider provides for a percentage of growth in the income account. This income account is used only for the purposes of calculating the income-payment amount when income is "turned on." The income account value is not available for withdrawal in a lump-sum amount.

For example, earlier in this chapter, we discussed a $100,000 annuity that grew to $271,809.57 after twenty years of 5 percent compound annual growth using the lifetime income-rider feature. The income that would be available would be calculated using the $271,809.57 annuity.

Guaranteed-Income-Payment Amounts

Different income riders offer different payouts. These are dependent on your age when you begin getting income, your sex, and whether you are taking a single payout or joint payout. Life-insurance companies employ actuarial tables to determine longevity, which influences the income payout percentage. Because younger people usually live longer than older people, younger retirees taking income payouts will usually receive a lower payment than older people.

The difference between a payout that begins at age fifty-five and one that begins at seventy-five could be two percentage points. For example, a fifty-five-year-old might receive a payout percentage of 3.5 percent while a seventy-five-year-old might get a payout of 5.5 percent. That would translate to a higher payout for the seventy-five-year-old and a lower payout for the fifty-year-year-old.

Besides age, payout factors also depend on gender. Because women typically live longer than men, they usually receive a slightly lower monthly benefit than a man of the same age. That difference depends on the insurance company and the specific type of product.

As I've mentioned, there is also the option for legally married couples to take a joint payout. Because that payout, in the case of a lifetime income payment, will last until the end of the life of the surviving spouse, those payout amounts are lower than individual payout amounts. On an actuarial basis, a joint payout is likely to last longer than the payout for an individual, which is why that income payout percentage is lower. There are advantages and disadvantages to both income payment options, and everyone's needs and objectives are different, but I usually ask that my clients consider the single payout and name their spouse as beneficiary. Then, under certain circumstances, the spouse may elect to continue income payments.

Payout and Rider Elections

After you purchase a fixed annuity product, you have many years and the potential to consult with your insurance agent or financial advisor before you have to decide whether to begin income. In most cases, I recommend a lifetime payout over a payout for a specific number of years. As I have noted earlier in this book, I always meet with my clients when they are getting ready to retire to discuss their retirement-income situation. It is during this conversation that this option comes up. This is an important conversation to have because once you decide on the payout period, that decision can't be changed.

Because there is no way to knowing how long you will live, a lifetime benefit is very attractive. Knowing that income will be available for life allows you to relax and enjoy your retirement. That income, along with a social-security benefit and income from a pension or other retirement sources, can complete the picture.

Required Minimum Distributions

Once you turn age seventy and a half, the Internal Revenue Service requires you to take required minimum distributions (RMDs) from your tax-deferred retirement accounts, such as your IRAs. If your fixed annuity is in an IRA, you may need to take higher payments than your contract's free withdrawal provision allows. In an effort to be as RMD friendly as possible, many insurance companies will increase your payment to meet the required amount for the amount of RMD attributable to the annuity. Typically this amount is not subject to surrender charge penalties.

Fees

Many insurance companies charge specific fees for riders such as lifetime income rider. Those fees are stated as a percentage of your accumulated value or income-rider value and are taken out of your contract automatically. You do not actually write a check for the annual fee.

CHAPTER 15
Client Case Studies

During the past forty-seven years, I have had the great fortune to work with some of the best clients a financial advisor could ever have. The financial products I sell are designed to protect my clients from risk. Risk is a funny thing. It's easy to dismiss the potential that whatever risks out there won't affect you—but there is no way to know.

That is exactly why products like life and disability insurance exist, to help you manage risks that you can't manage on your own. It is the same with fixed index annuities' longevity, and market risks are all out there. And you need to ensure that you have sufficient monthly income to meet your retirement needs. I believe so much in the products I sell because they fill such an important need for my clients. You never know when tragedy will strike, and I have attended more than one funeral for a client who died unexpectedly and before his or her time. When the widow or widower thanks me for the insurance that will provide the surviving family with worry-free income, tears fill my eyes. I never want to see my clients any less than happy, and I feel so much for these bereaved families because they have lost a loved one who can never be replaced.

In this chapter, I will walk you through some examples of common situations where the products can help people through difficult situations. It is so gratifying to me that I can help people in this way because it really makes a difference in their lives.

Fixed-Index-Annuity Case Studies
Case Study #1
Scenario: A couple in a golfing community in Florida was seeking more reliable ways to invest their retirement funds. They weren't happy with the answers that the advisors they approached suggested and didn't want to get any closer to retirement with their current level of risk.

Event: Friends of theirs recommended that they speak to me. They told the story of how I sold them a fixed index annuity and how much they liked my approach to providing products that offer reliable, guaranteed income in retirement.

Outcome: After several meetings with this couple, they purchased two large fixed index annuities, one for the husband and one for the wife. This purchase would ensure that they have sufficient guaranteed monthly income in retirement, so they could sleep well at night, which is the SWAN principle that I believe in so much.

Making a Difference: This couple told me, "You know, Bob, the reason we are doing business with you is because of this gentleman, our mutual friend. He told us how honest you are and how hard you work and how you follow up. We are very comfortable and would like to do what you recommend." I was so touched but not surprised as I treat each and every client with the respect they deserve.

Case #2
Scenario: The same couple, who reside in New Jersey as well, became excellent clients of mine. They were so pleased with their purchase that they recommended the same contract to their daughter.

Event: I flew from Pittsburgh to New Jersey to deliver the parents' two contracts, and my clients were thrilled that I was coming to deliver the contract in person. I believe in personal service and was glad to see them and spend the time with them. While I was there, we had a conversation about their other liquid assets and the best ways to employ those assets for the financial protection of their family.

Outcome: They decided to purchase the same kind of annuity from funds they had in a checking account for their fifty-year-old daughter. After the daughter's contract was issued, I drove to New Jersey again to deliver her contract in person.

Making a Difference: Not only will this couple experience financial protection in retirement, but their daughter will too. What a fabulous gift to give your child! At her age, with fifteen or twenty years of deferment, she will have income throughout her retirement, guaranteed for life!

Case #3
Scenario: Two successful business owners were enjoying the financial rewards that came with entrepreneurship. They didn't want to put the money they had worked so hard for at risk and wanted to ensure a comfortable future for their families.

Event: We were golfing buddies, and they approached me. We discussed their current situation, including their life insurance, and ways that they could ensure a reliable income during retirement after years of hard work.

Outcome: They purchased several fixed index annuities. Also, even though I did not sell them their life insurance or company pension plan, I had taken over servicing those products, and they were delighted with the quarterly reports and analysis that I provided them.

Making a Difference: They will be in a very strong position whenever they decide to retire. Each one of them will receive guaranteed, reliable income from the fixed index annuities they have purchased.

Disability-Insurance Case Studies
Case Study #1
Scenario: A resident physician purchased a disability-insurance policy to protect his family against an unexpected injury, illness, or incident that would interfere with his ability to work.

Event: In his late fifties, this surgeon became permanently disabled due to a coincidence of medical events, including back and knee surgery as well as a heart attack.

Outcome: The disability-insurance policy provided $7,000 a month tax free, through retirement age. This replaced the surgeon's income, ensuring that he could live comfortably and spend time on the rehabilitation he needs from his back and knee surgeries.

Making a Difference: My client told me, "I can't thank you enough." I believe in what I do and am so glad that the protection that this product provided has enabled my client to continue to pursue his lifestyle without worry.

Life-Insurance Case Studies
Case Study #1
Scenario: A close friend of mine throughout college purchased a life-insurance policy from me a few years after graduation.

Event: About fifteen years later, he contracted an illness in which he did not survive.

Outcome: The proceeds of the policy, tax-free dollars, allowed the widow to pay off her mortgage, send their children to college, and manage the family's financial affairs worry-free.

Making a Difference: At the funeral, the widow said to me, "You know something, you are the most important person here." How do you reply to something like that? I am glad, that in the midst of tragedy, I was able to help in some way that made a difference.

Case Study #2
Scenario: A medical student bought a life-insurance policy to provide for his mother in case of an untimely event.

Event: A few years after purchasing this policy, this young doctor became depressed and committed suicide.

Outcome: His mother received a check for $150,000, which I helped her roll over into an annuity, which grew to $220,000. At my recommendation, she then rolled it into a fixed index product, which she was very happy about.

Making a Difference: Although I never met this lady, she thanked me so many times. When I spoke to her after the funeral, she said, "Thank you so much."

We have maintained a relationship through the years and are in touch with birthday cards, letters, and phone calls.

Case Study #3

Scenario: A couple, both young doctors, were interested in gaining protection from potential tragedies that might derail their careers or result in untimely death.

Event: They decided to purchase several million dollars in whole life insurance to protect against tragedy and build cash value.

Outcome: Unexpectedly, the husband passed away in his fifties. The widow, still a practicing physician, was the beneficiary of the multimillion-dollar life-insurance policy. She rolled the proceeds over into a fixed index annuity and purchased several other annuities over the years to supplement her retirement income.

Making a Difference: I was friends with this couple for many years and maintained my friendship with the widow. She was so grateful that she not only had financial protection for herself and her children but also could afford to renovate her home through her ability to withdraw funds from the annuity without penalty.

CHAPTER 16
What Will Your Retirement Look Like?

Retirement presents numerous challenges. The financial piece is just one of them. Others include how you will occupy your time and where you plan to do that. All three are intimately connected, because each one affects the other. All too often, preretirees focus purely on the financial aspects of retirement and aren't fully prepared for the emotional, logistical, and lifestyle aspects.

I'm not knocking financial preparation—that is what this book is about. But if you haven't really considered how radically your life will change once you retire and how you will fill your time, you won't be prepared. And if you aren't fully prepared, your financial projects might not be on target. In other words, you might end up spending significantly more or less than you budgeted because your retirement lifestyle is different from what you anticipated.

Emotional Aspects
Most preretirees underestimate the emotional aspects of retirement. After all, for the vast majority of our lives, we've focused on either preparing for a career or building a career. For example, if you retire when you are sixty-five, odds are you spent at least seventeen years preparing to work (thirteen years of school plus four years of college). Many have spent longer—maybe even seven, eight, or nine years in a professional or graduate school and postgraduate training. Even if you've spent time out of the workforce, odds are you have some sort of vocation in the form of volunteer work or a hobby or pastime that you find absorbing. Either way, you've had a vocation or passion that you have pursued for most of your life.

Retirement means the end of much of that, especially for those whose lives have been absorbed by paid employment. That is essentially what retirement means—the end of paid employment. When so much of our emotional focus and validation has been expended in one area, it can be hard to manage the transition into finding a different type of emotional focus and validation. Before you retire, give this some thought. Consider what your emotional focus tends to center on and what it will be like to leave that behind. It may be a relief, or it may be a challenge—or both. If you give this some thought and acknowledgment before you retire, you will at least have some awareness if you feel emotionally off-balance as your retirement begins.

Managing those feelings isn't always easy. Building exercise in your routine can help, as can creating a routine for your days and your week. Structure helps ground whatever our experience of reality is. Talk to your spouse, if you have one, ahead of retirement and work on cocreating your experience and your schedules. If you feel down, share that rather than taking your feelings out on whoever happens to be around.

Logistical Aspects

While retirement doesn't have to mean the end of other hobbies or pursuits, it may radically change those pursuits. If, for example, an important part of your routine is civics clubs and activities such as yoga and exercise classes, how are you going to stay connected with those pursuits and friends if you are engaging in the passion of travel? While travel doesn't have to disrupt your schedule, the travel of young retirees I know—those in their sixties and early to midseventies—has the potential for disruption. When you are coming out of a long career that precluded extended trips, that is just what you are longing to do—really exploring the culture of another country. Add a two-week trip to China in the fall and a ten-day spring Mediterranean cruise with several trips to see friends and family and a weeklong stint with the grandkids, and you are talking about serious schedule impingement.

Many retired couples have to reimagine their retirement because two of their goals—volunteer work and travel—are incompatible. Typically, organizations need volunteers they can count on to fill scheduled and regular needs. That doesn't work out for those who travel frequently and/or spend part of their time in one place and the rest of the year in another. Snowbirds are a perfect example. If you spend five months in Florida and seven months in Michigan, how are you going to maintain your community ties, friendships, and pursuits? It's a challenge. That isn't to say it isn't doable, but putting some thought into it as you design your retirement will make it more possible than if you didn't expect it.

Your retirement could involve even more of a radical change—perhaps you are contemplating starting over somewhere else. You might want to sell the big house where you raised your family and move to a more hospitable part of the country. Or you might want to keep the family home and add a second home and become one of the snowbirds. These are big decisions that will have an impact on every part of your life as well as your finances. For those of us who are married, we need to make these decisions collaboratively.

Lifestyle Aspects

Obviously, where you live and the activities you pursue are important parts of your lifestyle. You need to think about what your daily routine and schedule will be like. If you don't have to get up and go to work, what will you do? Will you sleep in and have a leisurely breakfast while catching up on the news? Or will you still get up early and, instead of going to work, catch an 8:30 a.m. yoga class? If you are used to eating lunch out with colleagues, what will you have for lunch? Will you go out or stay in and eat leftovers? When will you fit your exercise in? How about your hobbies and socializing? There is a lot to think about.

Now I'm not suggesting that you create a spreadsheet and micromanage your days. All I'm saying is that it is a good idea to give some thought to all this before you pack up your desk and get your gold watch. You might want to plan some activities the first few weeks to ease the transition. Maybe even take that big trip right away. You don't have to answer every question or fill every minute of your time right away—you can evolve into an enjoyable retirement. That, like every other endeavor, is best undertaken with some thought and consideration.

Aligning Lifestyle with Finances

Before my clients retire, we have a conversation about their income in retirement. A big part of this is deciding when to start taking income from the deferred annuities that they have purchased. There are many other retirement-income variables, such as when to take social security. There may also be pension or investment income to consider as well.

As I've mentioned before, to get a handle on your postretirement income, monitor your preretirement income and expenses. It helps to have some kind of benchmark even if you end up making significant changes to your lifestyle. Think through your goals for retirement and at what point you might want to make significant changes in your lifestyle.

For example, if you want to start your retirement with a bang, such as a month-long trip to Southeast Asia, consider how you will fund the trip and how it may affect your retirement income and savings. That scenario could work out well if your regular monthly cash flow from other sources can handle your monthly expenses. Then you can wait for a few years to pull the trigger on monthly income from your annuity, allowing the annuity more time to grow so you have more principal to draw on over the length of your retirement.

Here's another scenario: you'd like to move to a warmer climate, a locale where one of your children has already relocated to with your grandchildren. However, you aren't exactly sure where in that area you want to live. Also, if you are going to move, you want to downsize significantly, which involves sorting through years of built-up clutter and mementos. That isn't a task you want to tackle fresh into retirement. So you decide to stay put for two to three years while you begin the process of getting rid of the clutter and taking periodic scouting trips to the new location. You can then create a budget for the relocation, remembering that now that you are retired, you won't have an employer subsidizing the move. You can build in all the anticipated expenses and decide when it would make sense to start drawing on your sources of income and in what sequence.

Or maybe now is the time to double down on your dream of golfing through your retirement. Perhaps you already live in a golfing community that you love, but you'd like some more variety. You might want to purchase a second home in another golfing community. That could involve a significant outlay of cash as well as ongoing golfing community fees. With proper planning, those expenses can be accounted for and built into a budget so that you won't spend more than your income.

I encourage you to explore the idea of a dream retirement. One of the saddest situations in retirement is where couples don't act on their dreams. For many, the failure to act on their dreams stems from the fear of running out of money. Research shows that when retirees are unsure of the stability of their monthly income due to the volatility of the stock market, their tendency is to underspend.[41]

---

41 Statman, "The Mental Mistakes We Make with Retirement Spending." (July 26, 2017)

That can lead to the lack of fulfillment. What have you worked so hard for? To fulfill your dreams, relax and enjoy this time in your life that you have worked so hard for and waited so long to achieve. Join my clients, many of whom are in the best situation possible headed into retirement—one where they have sources of monthly income due to fixed index annuities. That way, no matter what retirement lifestyle you want to pursue, you have income you can't outlive.

CHAPTER 17
Retirement-Income Flexibility

As you work through the front nine and enjoy the back nine, you come to understand how important adaptability and flexibility are both in a golf game and in your life. We've all experienced adversity, whether it's a ball in the rough or the water hazard or an illness or disability. When you possess financial flexibility, you can bounce back from adversity and maintain your standard of living even when times are tough.

No one is immune from difficulty. I've seen my clients go through plenty of it, and I have myself. Resilience characterizes those who are able to bounce back from adversity. Obviously, it helps to have a strong financial situation. That is how I've helped my clients through the years—by ensuring that their retirement savings is protected in the event of difficulties. That is the role of life insurance, disability insurance, and annuities.

Many of my clients were fortunate in that they never had the need for a life-insurance policy to pay benefits. Because they listened to my advice and purchased whole life instead of term, they had something of value to leverage when they didn't need life insurance anymore. It wasn't easy for these at the time young professionals to afford the type of coverage that they really needed, either for life or disability. But they persevered, making payments so that their families could be protected.

Then, as they moved ahead in their careers, they saved as much as they could, for retirement, for a college education for their children, and for a rainy day. Now those clients have amassed a significant amount of savings and are preparing for retirement. Because of their foresight and hard work, they have created a great deal of flexibility for themselves during retirement.

Let's look at a few scenarios and how it might work to sequence your income sources to maximize your flexibility during a thirty- to thirty-five-year retirement.

Sequencing Saving

Many high-net-worth individuals are fortunate enough to have liquid savings that can carry them through the first several years of retirement. Tapping into savings to support monthly income for the first few years of retirement has a number of advantages. You can postpone taking monthly income from social security and fixed index annuity so that those two sources of income are potentially larger.

Social security is available to individuals sixty-two years or older. The longer you wait to claim, the larger your benefit will be up to age seventy. There are claiming strategies that married couples can utilize to maximize their joint income. For instance, one could claim at full retirement age, which is currently sixty-six, while the higher earning spouse could postpone claiming until age seventy to receive the maximum benefit. So if a couple who both retired at age sixty-five lived on liquid savings for even one year before claiming the first spouse's social security, they would then receive an income stream from that first payment. That amount of income should reduce the amount of income they need to take from their liquid savings. Then, four years later, they could claim the second spouse's income. That might allow them to postpone drawing income from the annuity for another several years, which would allow to grow further.

Another option would be for both spouses to double down on social security and claim at full retirement age. That, along with liquid savings, could cover expenses for four or five years, at which time they could begin to receive monthly income from their fixed index annuity.

Multiple Deferred Annuities

Many of my clients have purchased multiple fixed index annuities, which offer even more flexibility. For example, if both husband and wife own annuity contracts, they could stagger when they start taking monthly payments. One could start taking monthly payments at sixty-eight and the other could begin at seventy-three. That would allow the second annuity to continue to compound over time, maximizing its overall value.

Many clients have more than two annuities. As I have mentioned, my wife and I own multiple annuities. This provides even more flexibility, as there are many options for taking one-time withdrawals and income from different products at different times. There are many reasons that you might want to purchase multiple annuities. First of all, it makes sense to purchase at least one for a husband and wife. That way each can have a distinct stream of income. Second, you may have different sums of money available at different times. Sources of funds for deferred income annuity purchase can include a pension or 401(k) plan rollover, an inheritance, proceeds from a business sale, exercise of stock options, or a bonus. Allocating those funds in a fixed index annuity keeps them from being spent and provides additional protection for your future income needs.

Many of my clients experience several of those events, which allow them to purchase annuities at different times. That can be very beneficial, especially as new annuity products are being released all the time. When new products come to market, I take the time to completely familiarize myself with them, analyzing them thoroughly to understand their features and benefits and how they compare to products already on the market. Some newer products offer advantages that other products don't have. Should some funds become available, you can take advantage of new features and really lock down your retirement needs.

When you combine multiple annuities with a pension, liquid savings, other investments, and social security, you have a powerful prescription for retirement-income protection.

Options for Single Retirees

If you are single, a fixed index annuity provides just as much flexibility as it does for married couples. In fact, retirement can be more challenging for those who are single than for married couples, because the expenses for single people are 80 to 85 percent as much as a married couple, but there is only one source of retirement income. Widows and widowers can benefit from their deceased spouses' social security and may be fortunate enough to also have life-insurance benefits.

Careful Planning Is Key

As I have mentioned, careful retirement-income planning is key. Understanding how you plan to live your life in retirement and what activities you plan to engage in gives you visibility into your expense patterns and income needs. Then, by matching your income to those needs, you can construct a retirement that maximizes your opportunities to enjoy the leisure and lifestyle you have worked so hard to achieve, while still benefitting from financial protection. It is the perfect prescription for the SWAN theory—sleep well at night.

CHAPTER 18

Financial Freedom

After a long round of golf, when you come to the eighteenth hole, it is great to find yourself in a winning position. Taking the round, shooting well, and feeling good all help make it a good day. Retirement is similar—after a long, rewarding career, it is wonderful to transition into a confident retirement. The biggest contribution to a confident retirement is financial freedom. When you know that you don't have to worry about how your bills are going to get paid every month, everything else falls into place.

Financial freedom brings complete financial flexibility. We've talked about how you might want to spend your time in retirement and where you might want to put your energy. Many retirees love spending time with their family, especially grandchildren. Traveling is high up on the list of many retirees as well. What isn't too far behind is philanthropy. Financial protection in retirement provides some space and scope to engage in philanthropy and to add that to your legacy. Many of us have a passion to give back or give to others. If you've been fortunate enough to sufficiently provide for yourself and your family, it can make sense to use your resources to impact your community for the good, in whatever form that might take.

Extending your financial freedom into future generations is a goal of many retirees. There are many different ways to do that. As I've mentioned, one of the best examples of providing for future generations is a client of mine who purchased a fixed annuity for their daughter. Her retirement is guaranteed. She now has a product that can provide guaranteed income for her retirement needs. What a terrific way to provide for your children. Purchasing a fixed index annuity for an adult child who is fifty or older can make the world of difference for their eventual retirement. Many of our children are burdened with educating their own children, paying for health-care costs, and managing their own careers. It isn't an easy balancing act, and by helping out on the retirement front, we can ease their burdens.

Your financial freedom can allow you to support your family in other ways. Perhaps you'd like to take your kids and grandkids on a Disney vacation—or a Disney cruise. Or maybe you want to support your children by helping pay private school tuition or a specialized summer camp for your grandchildren. Many grandparents, including my wife and myself, establish Section 529 Savings Accounts for their grandchildren's college education. It is not only a great way to help your children and grandchildren, but it also gets potentially taxable assets out of your estate. The gift of financial freedom that you've given yourselves makes these goals possible.

Ultimately, financial freedom and flexibility means that you can sleep well at night, the SWAN concept. There is no greater gift that you can give yourself and your spouse than a well-earned and reliable retirement income. If you've gotten anything out of reading this book, I hope that message has gotten through that proper planning that includes guarantees for retirement income can help you achieve your aspirations and financial goals. Purchasing a fixed index annuity can assist in achieving that state of mind.

If there is anything I can do to help you and your financial situation, please contact me at my office, Robert J. Duchin and Associates Ltd. at 724-392-4192. It has been my privilege during my career to work with so many wonderful clients. Thank you for reading this book.

This book is not intended to be legal or tax advice. The author can provide information, but not advice related to social-security benefits. Clients should seek guidance from the Social Security Administration regarding their particular situation. The author, a financial professional, may be able to identify potential retirement-income gaps and may introduce insurance products, such as an annuity, as a potential solution. Social-security-benefit-payout rates can and will change at the sole discretion of the Social Security Administration. For more information, please direct your clients to a local Social Security Administration office, or visit www.ssa.gov.

Advice

The statements and opinions expressed are those of the author and are subject to change at any time. This material has been prepared for informational and educational purposes only. It is not intended to provide and should not be relied upon for accounting, legal, tax, or investment advice.

Annuities are insurance products backed by the claims-paying ability of the issuing company; they are not FDIC insured; are not obligations or deposits of; are not guaranteed or underwritten by any bank, savings, and loan or credit union or its affiliates; and are unrelated to and not a condition of the provision or term of any banking service or activity. Annuities are long-term products of the insurance industry designed for retirement income. They contain some limitations, including possible withdrawal charges and a market-value adjustment that could affect contract values. This material only provides highlights of this product—please refer to the product disclosures for information regarding exclusions, limitations, and reductions of benefits and terms, including costs and complete details of coverage. Bonus annuities may include lower caps, higher spreads, or other restrictions that are not included in similar annuities that don't offer a premium bonus feature. Guaranteed lifetime income is available through annuitization or the purchase of an optional lifetime income rider, a benefit for which an annual premium is charged.

The Internal Revenue Code already provides tax deferral to IRAs, so there is no additional tax benefit obtained by funding an IRA with an annuity; consider the other benefits provided by an annuity, such as lifetime income and a death benefit.

Withdrawals from an annuity may have the effect of reducing the death benefit, living benefits, and/or cash surrender value. Withdrawals of taxable amounts are subject to income tax and may also be subject to a 10 percent IRS penalty tax if withdrawn before age fifty-nine and a half. Although qualified withdrawals from a Roth IRA are tax free, when converting a Traditional IRA into a Roth IRA, the entire converted taxable amount is reportable as income in the year of conversion.

The S&P 500® Index does not include dividends paid on the underlying stocks and therefore does not reflect the total return of the underlying stocks; neither the S&P 500® Index nor any market-indexed annuity is comparable to a direct investment in the equity markets. Indexed annuities do not directly participate in any stock or equity investments. Clients who purchase fixed index annuities are not directly investing in the S&P 500®.

The testimonials may not be representative of the experience of other clients and are no guarantee of future success. The testimonials were not paid for.

www.ingramcontent.com/pod-product-compliance
Lightning Source LLC
Chambersburg PA
CBHW070423240526
45472CB00020B/1168